YOU
are part of
a wonderful
WEB OF
LIFE.

The Kids' Book of Awesome Stuff

Charlene Brotman

illustrated by
Jeila Gueramian

Publushed by Brotman Marsh-Field Curriculums,
Biddeford, ME

Reordering information
Copies of the Kids' Book of Awesome Stuff may be obtained by contacting:
Lindy Anderson
brotmfcurr@aol.com
207-282-4539
or
Charlene Brotman
brotmanco@aol.com
617-332-5616

Permission to Reproduce Pages:
Permission is granted to educators to reproduce individual pages for the
purpose of deepening a child's sense of being part of a wonderful web of life.

Illustrations: Jeila Gueramian
Book Design: Susan B. Charles
Assistant Editor: Noreen Kimball

Library of Congress Control Number 2004097721
ISBN 0-9762568-0-0
Printed In Canada

Dedicated
to the memory of
Barbara Marshman and Ann Fields.
Together we envisioned this book.
I feel their presence in
every page.

Awesome Contents

Awesome Stuff #1

You're Made of
Star-Stuff

Did you know...
You wouldn't be alive today
if ancient stars had not died and blown apart?
Even Earth would not exist!

And did you know...
you're made of STAR-STUFF,
the chemical elements that were
once *inside* the stars that died?

Those exploding stars
hurled their elements out
into space in gigantic clouds of dust and gas.
Over time, some of the elements from
the stars formed the Earth and the Sun.
Some of that star-stuff ended up in
YOU!

That makes YOU
a STAR-KID from
outer space!

And I'm a
STAR-DOG!

A Blinding FLASH

The chemical elements you're made of, such as oxygen, iron, carbon, hydrogen, nitrogen, and calcium, are all star-stuff from outer space. Parts of stars are in your blood, your bones, your whole body.

Elements from stars make up everything on Earth, just as ingredients make up a cake. You and air, water and rocks, bacteria, beetles, and buzzards are created from these elements.

The story of the star-stuff that became YOU goes all the way back to the Big Bang, when the Universe began 14 billion years ago. It's a story about stars that were born, and stars that died.

First came the blinding flash of the Big Bang, and then the Universe was left pitch-black. No stars. No planets. No light. Nothing existed in the whole Universe, except for some gases that floated in the blackness. Those gases were mostly hydrogen and helium.

But in time, gravity pulled and crammed clouds of hydrogen and helium atoms together so tightly that they heated up. Atoms, the smallest pieces of an element, got squashed. The giant clumps of gas grew hotter and hotter. And then…they lit up.

The first stars in the Universe were born!

Stars Are Still Being Born!

Stars are born in clouds of hydrogen gas, such as this one, named N81. The white spots are young stars.

Stars are giant balls of glowing gases, mostly super-heated hydrogen. A star is a sun, and the Sun is a star.

Starlight and sunlight come from *nuclear fusion*, not from flames. Deep in the core of a star, where it's hottest, immense heat makes atoms fuse—join together—and become a different, heavier element. Hydrogen atoms change into helium atoms, and helium atoms join to form atoms of carbon and oxygen. The bigger the star, the hotter it gets, and the hotter it gets, the more kinds of elements it can make inside itself.

A star's fuel is hydrogen gas. When a star runs out of fuel, it is doomed to die.

Dying Stars Fling Stuff (elements) into space!

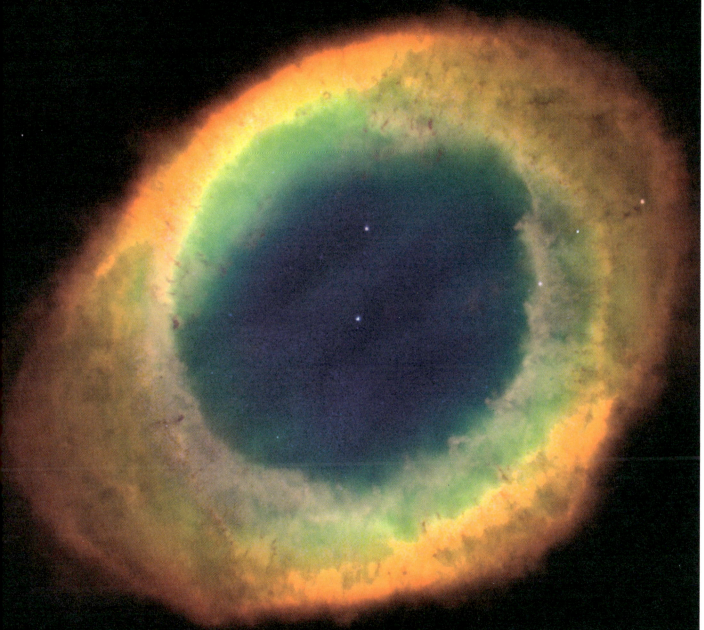

You are looking into a tunnel of hot gases blown off a dying star. This is called the Ring Nebula. In this photo the element helium is represented by blue, oxygen by green, and nitrogen by red. All that is left of this dying star is its core—the white speck in the center. The scattered white dots are other stars.

Doomed Stars

Medium-sized stars like our Sun puff off their outer layers when they die.
The glowing puff of gas is called a nebula. Each dies with its own kind of fireworks.

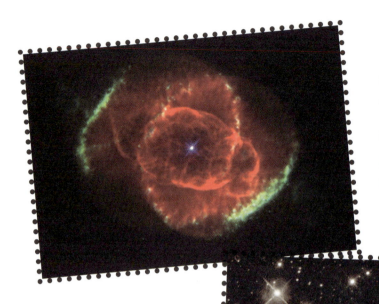

Cat's Eye Nebula
The point of light in the center is the dying star. It ejects its gases like a lawn sprinkler that twirls around and around.

Ant Nebula
The white spot in the center of the "ant" is the dying star. It ejects gases like two jet engines.

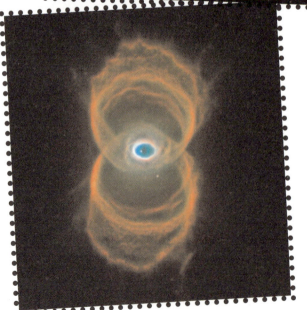

Hourglass Nebula
The reddish-orange rings of gas are nitrogen. The star's core—its nuclear furnace—is the white dot in the center.

Check it out
Our galaxy has more than a thousand dying stars!

Cygnus Loop supernova

When a *giant* star dies, it erupts and crashes in on itself. This is called a **supernova**. The titanic explosion instantly creates even more kinds of elements through nuclear fusion, such as gold, silver, lead, and tin. The photo above shows part of the Cygnus Loop supernova, which exploded 15,000 years ago. Its blast wave is still slamming into clumps of gas in outer space, heating the gas and making it glow.

Star-stuff gets recycled

in space. Elements from stars that died float in space for billions of years. Gravity recycles some of this floating star-stuff into new stars.

Did you know I'm recycled STAR-STUFF?

The star that is our Sun was born about 5 billion years ago. Then a disk of dust, gas, and elements spun around the newborn Sun. The spinning star-stuff clumped together to form nine planets, their moons, icy comets, and rocky asteroids. This is the Sun's family—the Solar System. You live on the third planet from the sun.

A star that lived and died before our Sun was even born made the calcium in your bones and teeth, and in egg shells and coral, moon rocks and marble.

An ancient star cooked up the carbon in your muscles, and in diamonds, moths, and mushrooms. Carbon from a star is in everything alive today.

And billions of years ago, a dying star created the iron that's in your blood right now, and the iron in comets and in the Earth's core.

Did you know? Scientists have discovered more than 100 moons in our Solar System!

You are related to everything else in the world, since you and all things come from the same star-stuff.

You're related to your favorite rock and your favorite sea shell. They're made of star-stuff, the same as you. You're related to green grass, lizards and thunder clouds—all from the same star-stuff.

I'm related to _____

(fill in the blank)

Lakota Native Americans say:

Mitakuye Oyasin

pronounced:
mee-DAK-oo-yay
o-yah-seen

We are all related

Mitakuye oyasin means "We are all related" in the Lakota language.

Lakotas believe that all people, animals, insects, trees, plants, birds, and rocks are our relatives. We are all related in a wonderful web of life on the Earth we share.

A Lakota person usually ends each prayer or speech by saying "Mitakuye oyasin!"

Awesome things can happen when elements hang out together. Guess what you get when one atom of a poisonous, greenish-yellow gas (the element chlorine) joins up with one atom of a silvery metal (the element sodium)? The answer is table salt or sodium chloride.

It's hard to believe, but atoms of a deadly gas and a metal combine to become something you sprinkle on your food.

When atoms of two or more elements join together, they turn into a *compound* that is totally different from those elements— almost like magic. Atoms of oxygen and silicon transform into sand when they combine. Sugar is made of carbon, oxygen, and hydrogen atoms.

Two gases make water!

Awesome!

Q: What do you get when two atoms of hydrogen, a gas, combine with one atom of oxygen, another gas? (Hint: it's not a gas.)

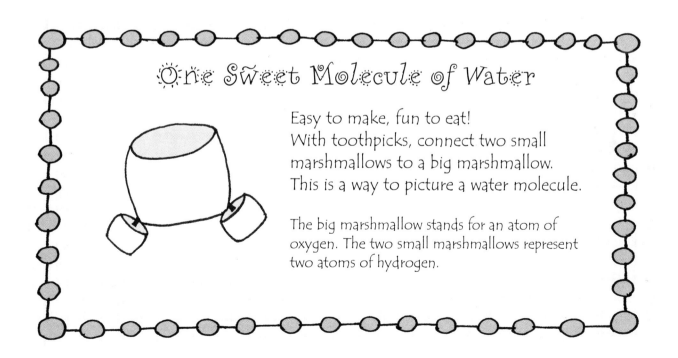

One Sweet Molecule of Water

Easy to make, fun to eat!
With toothpicks, connect two small marshmallows to a big marshmallow. This is a way to picture a water molecule.

The big marshmallow stands for an atom of oxygen. The two small marshmallows represent two atoms of hydrogen.

Since snowflakes are a form of water, they are also made of hydrogen and oxygen atoms. Just think, snowflakes have their beginnings in the blast furnace of a star.

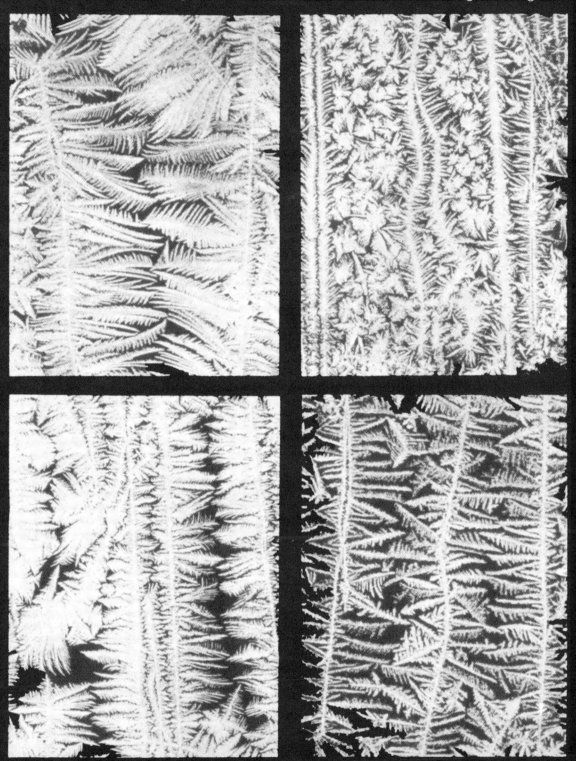

Frost is also made of hydrogen and oxygen from a star.

Did you know...a lot of YOU is also hydrogen and oxygen? One reason is that over half of your body's weight is water. You are mostly made of hydrogen, oxygen, and carbon, but you have small amounts of most of the other elements. The hydrogen in your body is as old as the beginnings of the Universe!

But how did elements from a star ever end up in ME?

And me?

The elements from stars that died never get used up or destroyed or lost on planet Earth. They just get **recycled.** Over and over. And finally, some ended up in YOU.

When any living thing dies, it decays and all of the elements that were combined together break apart. It is just as if you pulled a Lego™ construction apart until it goes back to all the little pieces you started with.

The elements that break apart from each other go into the air...or soil...or water. They may become part of rocks and clouds and oceans. Or they may become food for plants. Those plants become food for animals and people.

Then the animals, people, and plants die and decay, and the elements recycle all over again. Some of the recycled elements now make up your own body.

The Long, Long, Back-and-Forth Journey

The same elements that are now part of your body may once have been part of these:

Add something to the picture above that you think might have had elements that are now part of you.

On their journey, the elements recycle from living things to non-living things and back to living things, throughout the ages.

When you die, the elements in your body will journey on to become part of earth, or air, or another living thing.

And so that is the story—the story of how it came about that you are made of star-stuff.

You are alive today on this planet Earth, because of ancient, glowing stars. You're a Star-Kid from outer space! You're *awesome*.

Make Your Own
STAR-STUFF JOURNAL

Record All the Cool Things You Find in Nature!
All you need is a drawing pad, pen, or pencil and a curious mind.

A journal is a record of *your* experiences and ideas. Start by putting the date and place on your journal page. Now make quick sketches of the cool stuff you see, hear, and find outdoors. Look for colorful mushrooms, animal tracks, cobwebs, seed pods, flowers, and leaves. Look under old logs (be sure to replace them carefully), inside tree holes, and in puddles. *Whatever you sketch, it's made of star-stuff, the same as you!*

Sketching helps you to really notice details of an object, and to remember them better.

Once you start your journal, you'll find that you see many things you never noticed before. You see with "new eyes."

STAR-STUFF Word Search

Find the names of some of the elements that were once inside a star. The names go forward, backward, up, down and on the diagonal.

oxygen   nitrogen   iron   silicon
hydrogen   carbon   calcium   mercury
gold   iodine   helium   chlorine
copper   lead   sulfur

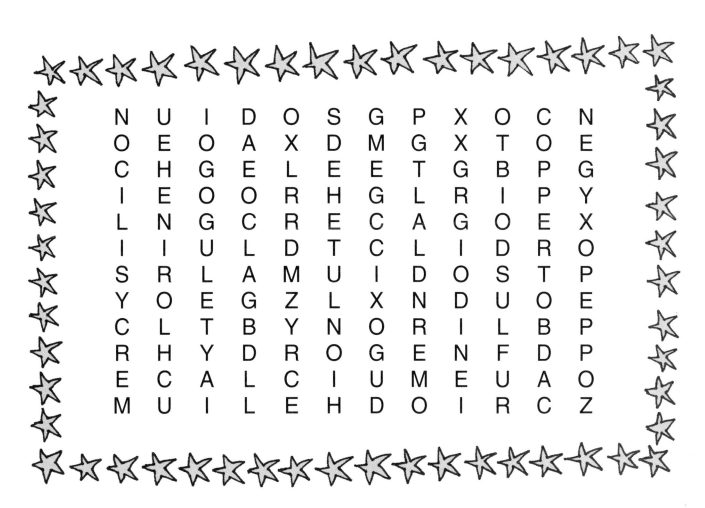

```
N U I D O S G P X O C N
O E O A X D M G X T O E
C H G E L E E T G B P G
I E O O R H G L R I P Y
L N G C R E C A G O E X
I I U L D T C L I D R O
S R L A M U I D O S T P
Y O E G Z L X N D U O E
C L T B Y N O R I L B P
R H Y D R O G E N F D P
E C A L C I U M E U A O
M U I L E H D O I R C Z
```

Tonight...

Go outdoors
and look at a star.

And look at your hands
and your whole self,
made of elements
that were once in a star.

How do you feel
about being a
STAR-KID?

You're Saved by Something Green

Take a deep breath. The air you just breathed *in* is different from the air you just breathed *out.*

Nitrogen, *Oxygen*

coming in

Nitrogen, *Carbon Dioxide*

going out

The air you breathed *out* is a gas that can suffocate you if too much of it gets in the air. That gas is carbon dioxide.

The oxygen you breathed *in* makes energy for you from the food you eat. But when your cells use the oxygen, they end up with something your body doesn't want: carbon dioxide. So your blood goes around to all your cells like a trash hauler, collecting the carbon dioxide and taking it to your lungs. You breathe it out.

All this goes on inside you!

All Night All Day...

...every creature on Earth

breathes out carbon dioxide. Over and over. That's a lot of suffocating gas!

I breathe out carbon dioxide!

Ssssoo do I!

Me too!

A little carbon dioxide in the air is normal and safe. But if the air around you filled up completely with carbon dioxide (or even just halfway), you would suffocate.

So...with all the breathing *out* that goes on in the world, what keeps you from smothering under a thick cloud of carbon dioxide?

What saves you?

You are saved by *something green*.

All over the planet, green plants on the land and in the ocean pull carbon dioxide gas out of the air by breathing it into themselves! The very same gas that can kill you is exactly what a green plant must have to live.

Plants don't breathe with lungs like yours, of course. Instead, they breathe in the carbon dioxide through millions of invisible holes on the underside of their leaves and on their stems. These tiny openings can close and open.

Every time a leaf breathes in carbon dioxide, it also breathes out an equal amount of pure oxygen. The leaf is getting rid of oxygen it doesn't want.

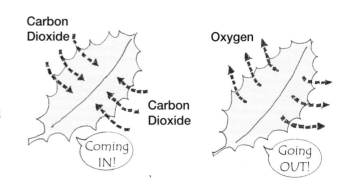

Carbon Dioxide

Carbon Dioxide

Coming IN!

Oxygen

Going OUT!

The same oxygen that leaves breathe out is exactly what you need to breathe in. You can't live without it. You breathe in what leaves breathe out. So do slugs. So do crows, crocodiles and crickets…

Oxygen from plants travels on wind currents from far-away continents and oceans. It reaches you even when the trees around you have lost their leaves, or if you live in a place with no leaves at all. Right this minute, you may be breathing in oxygen from a rain forest in Costa Rica, or a field of red poppies in Turkey.

if Every Plant on the Planet Disappeared...

Night-Breathers
for Your Bedroom

Most plants give off oxygen during the daytime, but a few kinds give off oxygen AT NIGHT!

Night-breathing plants are perfect for your bedroom, because they put oxygen into the air around you while you sleep, and take away the carbon dioxide you breathe out. The snake plant and aloe vera plant are two night-breathers that are really easy to grow. Here's how:

Aloe vera

This plant's amazing goo heals burns, sunburn, and scrapes. Just break off a piece of leaf. Clear goo will ooze out. Put the goo on your skin. Aloe vera has been used for healing for over 3,000 years.

Light: Two to five hours of direct sunlight a day.

Water: Let soil dry out between waterings. In winter, only water lightly.

Plant food: Give it plant food once a month in spring and summer, but do not feed it in fall and winter.

Snake plant:

Its stiff, spear-like leaves grow two to four feet high.

Light: The snake plant is not fussy about light. It can grow in a dim room or a bright one.

Water: Water lightly, only when the soil is dry. Over-watering a snake plant can cause its roots to rot.

Plant food: Give it a little plant food about once a month.

Brain Twister: What has no mouth, but makes it own food? answer on page 26

The Secret Goings-On inside a Leaf

As Told By A Dandelion Leaf

I'm just a dandelion leaf, but I can SPLIT WATER!

You can't see me split water, but I do. I do it inside myself. My dandelion roots pull in water from the ground. I split the water, and PRESTO! The water isn't water, anymore. I've changed it into invisible gases. You'd think I was some kind of green magician, instead of a dandelion growing in a crack in the sidewalk.

As I guess you know, a water molecule is made of two atoms of hydrogen that are joined to an atom of oxygen. I split the hydrogen atoms in water apart from the oxygen atoms. That turns the water back into the gases it's made of.

I catch the sun energy with my own solar panel, a green chemical called chlorophyll (pronounced KLOR-uh-FILL).

After I split water into hydrogen and oxygen, I only keep the hydrogen. I need it for making food. The oxygen is just waste, a leftover from splitting water, so I breathe most of it out into the air.

Sunlight travels 93 million miles to reach a leaf.

But there's more secret stuff going on that you can't see. Inside me, the hydrogen joins together with the carbon dioxide that I breathe in. And then…more magic! They stop being gases. They turn into sugars and starches and other chemicals. That's the food my dandelion plant uses for growing, and making seeds and yellow blossoms and roots.

Just to look at me, a little dandelion leaf, you'd never guess that I can breathe in carbon dioxide, split water, and turn gases into food. But all this goes on inside me. It goes on inside each blade of grass, each pine needle, each rose leaf. Every leaf you see performs all that secret, invisible chemistry!

Only we leaves can create food by putting together hydrogen from water, carbon dioxide from air, and energy from sunlight. It's called photosynthesis (pronounced: foe-toe-SIN-thuh-sis). And now you know some of my secrets!

No way you HUMANS can make food out of air, sunlight, and water!

You've gotta be GREEN to do it!

LEAF SCAVENGER HUNT!

FIND:

[ ] A leaf with a very smooth edge
[ ] A leaf with a zigzag edge
[ ] A leaf that feels fuzzy or rough
[ ] A leaf that catches a lot of sunlight
[ ] A leaf shaped like a needle
[ ] A leaf that has a flat stem
[ ] A leaf that is your favorite
[ ] A leaf shaped like a hand with the fingers spread out

Leafy bits of information:
Fuzz keeps moisture in the leaf
Bigger leaves catch more sunlight
Leaves with flat stems move easily in the wind

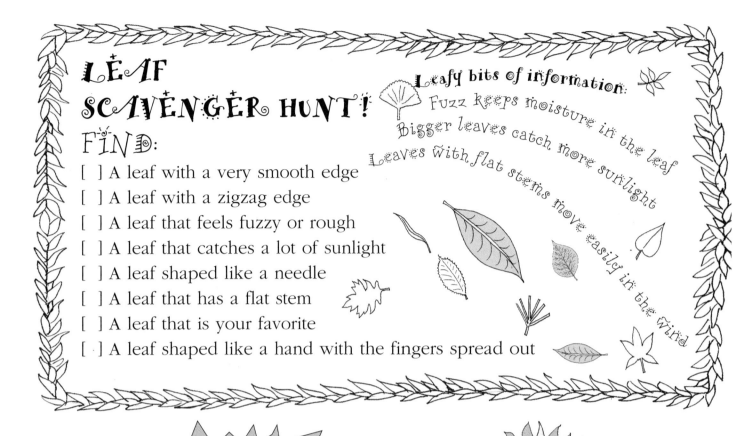

Leaf Match Hunt!

Draw or trace leaves growing in your neighborhood. Give each scavenger player a copy, and send them out to bring back leaves that match your drawings.

Leaves are awesome!

Brain Twister Answer: A plant!

SUPER-LEAF SCRAMBLE

Every leaf is a SUPER leaf. Rearrange the large letters to make a word that fits the sentence.

1. A 🍃 can TPISL _ _ _ _ _ water into oxygen and NOHEGRDY _ _ _ _ _ _ _ _ .

2. 🍃🍃 save you from a GSA _ _ _ that could ROTMHES _ _ _ _ _ _ _ you.

3. 🍁🍂 put GNXEYO _ _ _ _ _ _ into the air that you breathe.

4. A 🍃 turns hydrogen and NRAOCB _ _ _ _ _ _ XIDEODI _ _ _ _ _ _ _ into sugars and starches.

5. 🍂🍃 use air, water and ISGUNTHL _ _ _ _ _ _ _ _ to make food for the plant. It's food for you, too. You eat the plant or you eat the animals that eat the plant.

Try This Some Nice Day...
Breathing With Trees

Lie on the ground under a tree.
Look up at the leaves.

Breathe in deep breaths.
Slowly breathe out.
Look up at the tree,
and think about this:

The air you breathe in
is breathed out by the tree.

The air you breathe out
is breathed in by the tree.

From the tree to you,
From you to the tree.

You and the leaves…
the leaves and you.

Back and forth…
Forth and back…

Over and over…
the Breath of Life.

The Awesome Thing About Poop and Pee And Dead Stuff That Rots

HOW FISH ARE SAVED FROM POISONING THEMSELVES

The poop and pee...

...of fish, grasshoppers, bats, owls, porcupines, and people—*all* poop and pee—has something in it more precious than diamonds or gold. It's...**Nitrogen!**

You can live without diamonds or gold, but you can't live without nitrogen. No plant or animal can survive without it.

> You can buy my great poop in garden stores!

Of course, nitrogen is in the air all around you, but your body can't use it, even though you breathe it in and out with every breath. No creature on Earth can take in nitrogen from air, and neither can any plant. **But...plants can get nitrogen from poop and pee!**

You get your nitrogen by eating plants...or by eating animals that ate plants.

Why You and Plants Can't Get Nitrogen from the Air

A molecule of nitrogen is made of two atoms of nitrogen stuck tightly together. Lightning can split those nitrogen atoms apart in the air. Rain washes them into the ground, and plants then take them in through their roots. But it's bacteria, not lightning, that split most nitrogen atoms. The kind of bacteria that can do this live in soil and water, and even inside the roots of some plants. These tiny, invisible bacteria are as powerful as lightning!

> You can't use us until...

> we atoms are SPLIT APART from each other!

a molecule of nitrogen

A New Way to Think About Poop

You can decode this message by holding it up to a mirror.

Nothing in is ever wasted in nature, not even poop and pee. Poop and pee give nitrogen to plants. Plants give nitrogen to Animals. Animals poop and pee. So nitrogen recycles from poop and pee to plants to animals and back again.

The way it all works is COOL!

That's bird poop...WOW! it's NITROGEN!

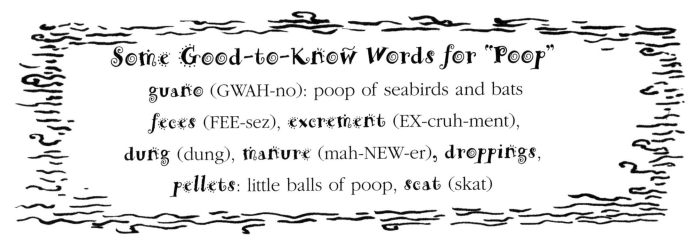

Some Good-to-Know Words for "Poop"

guano (GWAH-no): poop of seabirds and bats

feces (FEE-sez), **excrement** (EX-cruh-ment),

dung (dung), **manure** (mah-NEW-er), **droppings**,

pellets: little balls of poop, **scat** (skat)

What has 6 legs and scoops up poop?

ME! A dung beetle!

Dung beetles scoop up animal dung, roll it into balls, bury the balls in the ground, and then lay their eggs in them. The buried dung balls become safe homes and fast-food restaurants for the larvae (from the eggs). The dung balls also put nitrogen into the earth where plant roots can take it in. If the dung had been left to rot on the ground, its valuable nitrogen would have escaped into the air.

I can roll a ball walking BACKWARD!

Just YOU try it!

The biggest kind of dung beetles eat elephant dung. They can roll balls of dung the size of croquet balls. Millions of years ago, dung beetles cleaned up after dinosaurs.

Can you imagine the size of those pooper-scoopers?

A True Story about WAY Too Much Cow Manure

Cows had never lived in Australia until new settlers decided to raise cattle. BUT… the dung beetles in Australia were not the kind that could handle heaps of cow manure. Those beetles had never buried anything bigger than the little dry pellets of kangaroos. Soon the cow manure piled up, choking the grass and plants underneath, and breeding swarms of blood-sucking flies. Finally, a settler from Hungary remembered the dung beetles on his farm back in Europe.

"That's it!" he thought. "Australia needs the kind of dung beetles that are right for cows." So the settlers brought in dung beetles from Europe and Africa, and the big poop problem was solved!

Yet More Stinky Stuff

And here's why: If nothing rotted, everything that ever died would still be here. Dead bodies and carcasses would pile up everywhere. There would be no room for an animal to be born, or even for a blade of grass to grow.

If nothing rotted, your world would look like this:

But even worse than running out of room: the world would run out of elements. If dead things did not rot, all the elements they are made of would just stay locked up inside them. Forever. Never to recycle. Without recycling, elements would have been used up long, long before *you* had a chance to be born.

Rotting unlocks the elements. Rotting frees the elements to recycle into babies and bumblebees and new life.

We Recycle Dead Stuff

We recycle dead stuff by helping it rot. We're little, but we keep the world running. Bacteria and fungi do most of the work, but the rest of us break dead stuff down to a size bacteria and fungi can attack. Can you find all of us recyclers in the word-search? The words can go up, down, side-to-side, diagonally and backward.

M	U	S	H	R	G	U	B	L	L	I	P	B
U	R	M	S	N	A	S	N	A	I	E	E	A
S	E	O	O	M	I	L	L	I	P	E	D	E
L	E	O	W	O	R	U	I	U	T	T	E	A
I	L	R	T	H	E	C	C	L	G	L	N	L
C	T	H	M	I	T	E	R	M	I	T	E	I
H	E	S	N	A	C	R	A	C	O	O	M	A
E	E	U	N	N	A	I	A	N	S	L	U	N
N	B	M	T	A	B	L	I	E	S	L	D	S

EARTHWORM	BACTERIA	TERMITE
BEETLE	LICHEN	MILLIPEDE
SNAIL	MOLD	SLUG
PILLBUG	ANT	MUSHROOM

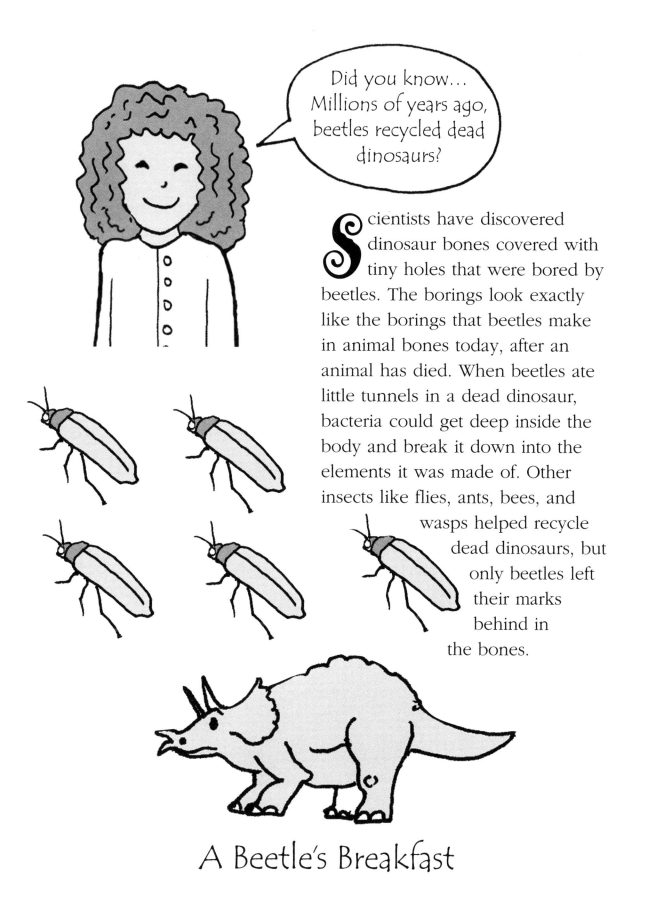

Did you know...
Millions of years ago,
beetles recycled dead
dinosaurs?

Scientists have discovered dinosaur bones covered with tiny holes that were bored by beetles. The borings look exactly like the borings that beetles make in animal bones today, after an animal has died. When beetles ate little tunnels in a dead dinosaur, bacteria could get deep inside the body and break it down into the elements it was made of. Other insects like flies, ants, bees, and wasps helped recycle dead dinosaurs, but only beetles left their marks behind in the bones.

A Beetle's Breakfast

Which Recycler Am I?

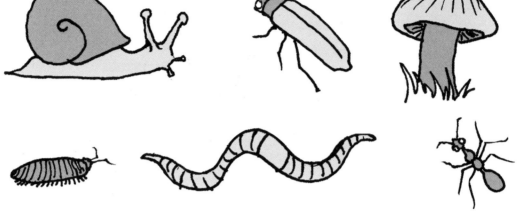

1. I eat, but I don't have a mouth or a stomach. I make a chemical that's powerful enough to turn a dead tree into crumbly soil. *Draw a line to one of the recyclers above.*

   I am a _____.

2. I eat a lot of dead leaves and dirt. I breathe through my damp skin. I have no legs, but I do have feet like tiny bristles. *Draw a line to one of the recyclers above.*

   I am a _____.

3. My tiny hooked teeth are all on my tongue. I like eating dead leaves and plants. My eyes are perched on the tips of stalks that stick up from my head. *Draw a line to one of the recyclers above.*

   I am a _____.

Upside Down Answers

1. I AM A MUSHROOM.
My powerful chemicals break down dead things into their elements, which I then soak up for lunch. What I don't eat goes into the soil, so the lucky plants living nearby feast on the leftovers. I need dead things to eat, because I can't make my own food like plants do. The part of me that makes the strong chemicals is hidden. It looks like lacy, white threads. You can spot them if you pry up a piece of bark on an old log. These tiny, delicate threads can digest a huge, dead tree! It takes a bit of time, of course. My threads are not roots, like roots on a plant. I'm not a plant, I'm a fungus. (The word for more than one fungus is fungi (FUN-ji).

2. I AM AN EARTHWORM.
When I burrow through soil, I eat dirt and dead leaves which pass through my body, mix with chemicals, and come out my other end as tiny pellets called

Hang in there, feet!

"castings." These castings are rich in the elements that plants need, like nitrogen, phosphorus and potassium. I change dead leaves and dirt into super-rich plant food! I absorb oxygen through my damp skin, but if I dry out, I cannot take in the oxygen, and I will suffocate. My feet are very tiny bristles on the bottom and sides of my body. They help me turn and move. When a bird tries to pull me out of the ground, I hang onto the walls of my burrow with my bristle-feet! See page 38 for more about worms.

3. I AM A SNAIL.
My teeth can cut, grind, and shred even the toughest vegetation like tree bark. I chew on rocks to get minerals. If you are very quiet, you may be able to hear a crunching sound when I eat. I leave a trail of sticky mucus that protects me from sharp things. It also helps me climb up and down and cling upside down. See more about snails on page 39.

Want to learn more about the Amazing Earthworm?
Try Worm-Watching...

You will need:

Earthworms
Look under damp, decaying leaves and rotting logs.

Magnifying glass

Clear glass dish
such as a glass pie plate.

Spray bottle
or drops of water to keep the worm moist

Damp paper towel

Sheet of paper

I see its insides!

Cool!

Keep me moist or I will suffocate

1. Put the worm on the glass dish.

2. Hold the dish above you in good light, so you can look at the worm from below. Look for its blood vessels and the long food tube inside its body.

Please: put me back when you are through worm watching.

3. Put the worm on the damp paper towel and look at it with your magnifying glass. Can you see the worm's bristle-feet?

4. Put the worm on a sheet of paper and listen very carefully. You may be able to hear the scratching noise of the worm's bristle-feet as it moves.

A Recycler You Can Keep as a Pet

You can find a snail by looking in damp, shady places, under stones, logs, or rotting leaves. Try snail-hunting at night with a flashlight.

You can make a snail house by getting an old fish tank, a large glass planter or other container. Put in about four inches of soil, a piece of grass sod, some stones, and bark. Add some white chalk or egg shell, so the snail will have calcium to make its shell. Use a small bottle cap to hold water for the snail. It could drown if the water holder is too large. Sprinkle or spray the soil with water to keep it moist. Keep the snail's home in the shade.

You can feed your snail dead leaves. Also try lettuce, but be sure to wash it first, in case it has insecticide on it.

Look at your snail with a magnifying glass. Put it on clear plastic or glass that you hold up so that you can watch it move from underneath. Also watch it climb up an overturned paper cup.

If you have several snails some might mate and lay eggs. Keep the newly hatched snails separate from the other snails. A snail is both a male and female at the same time, so it produces both eggs and sperm. Still, it needs to mate with another snail before it or the other snail can lay eggs.

You Can Invite an Invisible Recycler to Dinner

Invisible mold spores float in the air, just waiting for the right spot to land to catch a good meal. A mold breaks its food down with chemicals, and then soaks up the elements, like mushrooms do. Molds and mushrooms are both fungi. Both grow from spores, not seeds.

You can make these invisible spores become visible by inviting them to dinner.

You can't see us...

but we float in the air...

all around you!

Here's How to Fix a Mold's Meal:

You will need

Food, such as a lemon, bit of jelly, slice of boiled potato, a piece of cream cheese, strawberries or bread with no preservatives in it.

Containers that can be sealed, such as glass jars with lids, or plastic bags that "zip" or have twist ties. You need one container for each kind of food.

What to do:

1. Put a piece of food in each container. Put a few drops of water on each food. Molds love moisture.

2. Wait about half an hour, and then seal each container. You can't see the mold spores, but they are lurking in your containers.

3. Put them in a dark closet or drawer for a week. Check on them every day if you wish. The longer they are left to grow, the more interesting they become. They can get really interesting!

I'm feasting on this lemon, but...

I'm also making poison to kill off...

BACTERIA that want my lemon dinner!

How many kinds of spores came to your dinner? What colors are they? Are they black? Bluish green? Pink, orange, or reddish? Look at your molds with a magnifying glass. The fuzz you see is a tangle of thread-like tubes that break down the piece of food into its elements and digest them. You may see tiny round "fruits" sprouting from the threads. The fruits make the invisible mold spores that go floating off into the air, ready for your invitation to din-

Recycling Elements
A Matter of Life & Death

If HUMANS suddenly VANISHED from Earth, life on the planet would go on. But life on Earth would end without the:

_____ and

_____, and

_____, and

_____, and other recyclers that

help make dead things _____.

key for decoding:

a	b	c	d	e	f	g	h	i	j	k	l	m	n

o	p	q	r	s	t	u	v	w	x	y	z

The Rose and the Garbage

ner.

A famous Buddhist teacher from Vietnam, named Thich Nhat Hanh (Tik-not-hawn), said:

In the garbage
I see a rose.
In the rose,
I see the garbage.
Without one,
the other cannot be.

When a beautiful rose wilts and dies, it becomes garbage. Then the garbage decays and makes the garden soil rich, so more roses can grow.
The garbage is transformed into the rose.

Just think . . . death and decay make new life possible.

Every living thing has an end.

Each of us must die someday.
That is the way of nature.

To be ALIVE
is a PRECIOUS GIFT.

So let's celebrate each new day
and say good morning to the sun!

A Yoga Salute to the Sun

Try this with a friend on a
bright sunny morning

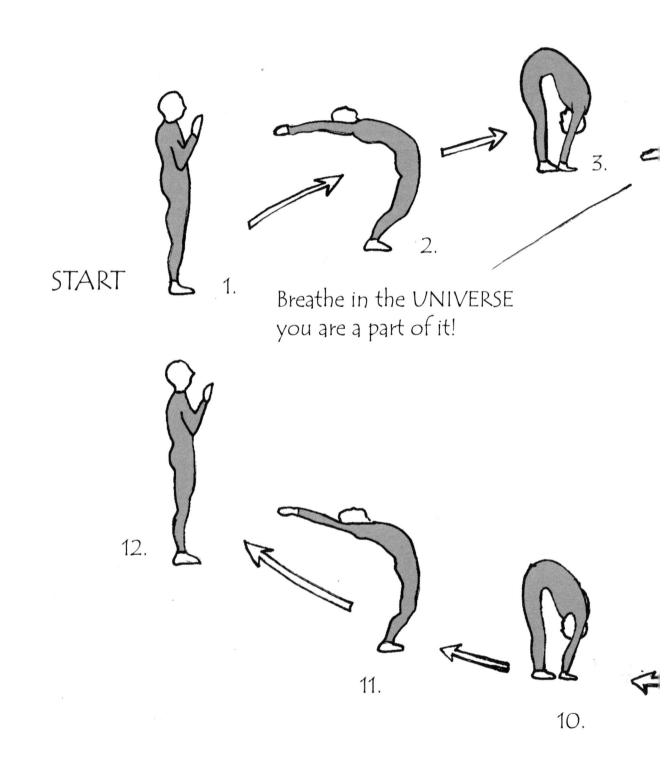

START

1.

2.

3.

Breathe in the UNIVERSE
you are a part of it!

12.

11.

10.

Use your body
instead of words

A WAY
TO SAY
THANK
YOU TO
LIFE!

4.

5.

6.

Feel your whole body
belonging to the earth

7.

8.

9.

What is it that a star and a nitrogen atom both do?
Color in the spaces with the dot
in them to find the answer.

First: if there were no bugs...

...most trees, plants, flowers and fruit would DISAPPEAR from the planet.

That's because most plants and trees cannot make seeds for new plants unless insects pollinate them.

When insects pollinate plants, they carry powdery pollen from the male part (anther) of a flower to the female part (pistil) of another flower. Then the flower can make seeds.

Bees, moths, wasps, ants, and butterflies pollinate plants. So do certain kinds of flies and beetles.

Ball of Pollen

Ball of Pollen

And next, if there were no bugs...

Many birds would disappear, because they would starve without bugs to eat. Other kinds of birds would starve without the seeds, nectar, and fruit of the plants that insects pollinate.

And then, if there were no bugs...

Frogs, turtles, lizards, snakes, bats, cats, cows, other creatures and people would disappear, because they eat insects, or they eat the plants that insects pollinate, or they eat the animals that eat the plants that insects pollinate.

So, if there were no bugs... What would be left on Earth?

Only grasses and a few trees and bushes that are pollinated by the wind.

I'd rather have bugs!

Bad Bugs or Good Bugs?

Of all the different kinds of bugs in the world, how many kinds are bad for us humans?
[ ] Most kinds of bugs are bad for us.
[ ] About half are bad.
[ ] Only a few kinds are bad.

ANSWER: ONLY A FEW KINDS OF INSECTS, ABOUT 1 1/2% ARE BAD FOR PEOPLE.

Good Stuff about Bugs

They do more than **pollinate** and **make meals** for other creatures. Some **eat dead plants and animals**, which helps put elements back into the soil for new plants. Some **bury animal dung.** Some **loosen up the soil** as they burrow in the ground, letting air and water reach the roots of plants. This is important because loose soil soaks up water for plants, but water runs right off of hard-packed soil.

Some Good Bugs That Eat Bad Bugs (Bad for people, that is)

Dragonfly

This fierce hunter can devour several hundred mosquitoes in one day.

Ladybug

It eats tiny aphids that can suck the life out of a plant. A single ladybug can eat 100 aphids a day.

Lacewing

It hunts insects, such as whiteflies, that eat plants we need for food. It has golden eyes!

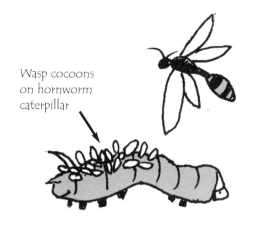

Wasp cocoons on hornworm caterpillar

Wasps

Some kinds lay their eggs in caterpillars that harm food crops. When the eggs hatch, the wasp babies, called larvae, eat the caterpillars.

Praying Mantis

It nabs flies and other insects with its forelegs that grip like tweezers.

THE BAD NEWS: When people spray bug killer poisons, called insecticides, good insects are killed along with the harmful insects.

MORE BAD NEWS: When birds eat the poisoned insects, they die, too.

Creature Feature

Pick me. I'm awesome!

What is the strongest creature in the world for its size?

a) gorilla

b) rhinoceros beetle

c) elephant

Answer: b. For its size, the rhinoceros beetle can carry a heavier load than any other creature in the world. It can hold 100 times its own weight!

If you were as strong as the strongest creature, how many pounds could you carry?

Your weight_____ x 100 = _____ pounds you could carry.

Go Buggy
On a Bug Safari

Fascinating bugs live right outside your own front door...

Hi there!

GOOD THINGS TO HAVE ON YOUR SAFARI:

- Magnifying glass
- Plastic jar with cloth for a lid, held on with a rubber band
- Sketch book and pencil for drawing bugs. Drawing helps you notice things about them, like the number of legs, and where those legs attach to the body. Use your sketches later to look up their names in a bug book.

WHERE TO HUNT:

1. Check under rocks, and damp leaves. Be sure to put the rocks back in the same place — they're somebody's home.

2. Pick apart a rotten log with a stick. Peel off a strip of loose bark. Poke around the crumbly wood.

3. Look for caterpillars on leaves with holes, or look in gauzy webs in trees.

4. Drag a butterfly net on a handle back and

forth through tall grass and wild flowers.

5. Go to a pond. You might see a water strider walking across the water, searching for water fleas. Make a bug scoop by tying a kitchen strainer to a long stick, and scoop through the water and the muck on the bottom. Put your catch in more of the same water in a light-colored pan and watch for movement.

6. On a midsummer or autumn night, take a flashlight and see if you can locate an insect in the grass or shrubs by listening for its chirping. You may track down a male cricket or katydid "singing" to attract a mate. A female katydid can hear the male's call from a mile away.

7. Dig in the ground.

8. Mash up a rotten banana and add a bit of orange juice to make it more gooey. Smear it with your hand on the bark of a tree. Return to the tree after dark with a flashlight. What insects are dining at night on your banana feast? You might see some moths.

BUG SMART TIPS

When you're through watching a bug in your jar, put it back where you found it. Handle the bug gently, or try not to handle it at all. Don't let the jar get in the sun because the heat can kill your bug.

continued…

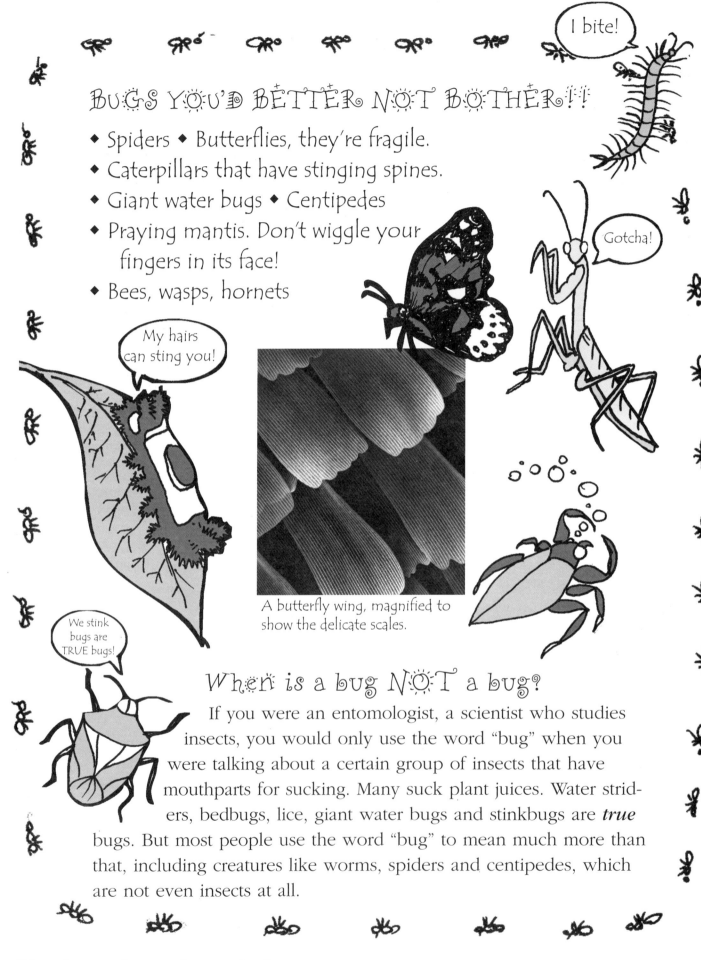

BUGS YOU'D BETTER NOT BOTHER!!!

- Spiders ◆ Butterflies, they're fragile.
- Caterpillars that have stinging spines.
- Giant water bugs ◆ Centipedes
- Praying mantis. Don't wiggle your fingers in its face!
- Bees, wasps, hornets

I bite!

Gotcha!

My hairs can sting you!

We stink bugs are TRUE bugs!

A butterfly wing, magnified to show the delicate scales.

When is a bug NOT a bug?

If you were an entomologist, a scientist who studies insects, you would only use the word "bug" when you were talking about a certain group of insects that have mouthparts for sucking. Many suck plant juices. Water striders, bedbugs, lice, giant water bugs and stinkbugs are **true** bugs. But most people use the word "bug" to mean much more than that, including creatures like worms, spiders and centipedes, which are not even insects at all.

A Strange Tale
Cats, Rats & Bugs
in Borneo
It Really Happened!

It all started with mosquitoes and flies.

The kind of mosquitoes on the hot, steamy island of Borneo can infect people with malaria, a deadly disease. The mosquitoes breed in Borneo's swamps and rainforests. So some years ago, the World Health Organization decided to get rid of the mosquitoes by spraying the island with great quantities of an insect poison called DDT.

Soon after the spraying, a weird thing happened: the thatched roofs of houses

began collapsing.

Hundreds of caterpillars were devouring the roofs. There had always been caterpillars around, but not many, because a certain kind of wasp ate them. But the DDT killed the wasps along with mosquitoes. The caterpillars were not affected much by the DDT. So, without wasps to stop them, they munched and crunched and chewed up the roofs.

But that is only the beginning of this tale. DDT was also sprayed inside the houses to kill houseflies. Now, killing houseflies had always been the job of little lizards called geckos. Geckos can scoot up and down walls and cling to ceilings when they hunt for flies, because they have tiny suction pads on the bottom of their feet. People in Borneo liked having geckos running around inside their houses, gobbling up insects. They always said that a gecko brings good luck.

The DDT killed houseflies, just as the World Health Organization had planned. But geckos ate the dead houseflies and then *they* died too, from the DDT in the bodies of the flies.

Then house cats ate the geckos. The poor cats died from the DDT

meow!

new cats into Borneo to catch the rats!

Geckos, cats, rats and roofs! And to think it all started with mosquitoes and flies.

By the end of this true tale, people discovered this: Each thing that happened made something else happen, because all living things are connected like the strands in a web—A WEB OF LIFE!

We can learn good ways to protect ourselves from the few kinds of harmful insects, BUT…

inside the flies inside the geckos.

After that, rats sneaked into houses, because there were no cats around to stop them. They ate up people's food. Worse than that, some of the rats carried a disease that was even more deadly than malaria.

This alarmed the World Health Organization so much that finally they parachuted

But folks are still messing up the environment when they try to get rid of bugs!

Read "No Peace in Keeping Silent" to find out more.

No Peace
in Keeping Silent

How Rachel Carson Helped Save the World
by Telling the Truth About Chemicals that Kill

A young Rachel reads to her dog, Candy.

Rachel Carson was a shy little girl, who played mostly by herself. No other children lived near the farm in Pennsylvania where she grew up.

TV and computers hadn't been invented when she was born in 1907, but Rachel was never bored. She loved wandering with her dog through the woods and streams on the farm, discovering snakes and birds, insects, and wild animals.

Sometimes she found fossils of fish and sea shells in the cliffs behind the farm, and tried to imagine the ancient sea that once covered the land.

When Rachel grew up, she was determined to go to college, even though most women at that time did not do that. Her parents were poor, but they sold the family china and some farm land so that she could go.

At first, the other students thought Rachel was snobbish, because she kept to herself. But then they realized she was just shy, and could be a good friend.

When Rachel decided she wanted to be a scientist, her friends at school said, "You can't! Only a man can be a scientist." Even the president of her college thought that women did not have the strength and brains to be scientists. That was how most people thought in those days.

Rachel decided to become a scientist, though everyone told her that was a man's job..

But Rachel took a test to work as a marine biologist and writer for the U.S. Fish and Wildlife Service. It had never hired a woman before. She scored higher than any of the men taking the test, and got the job.

She was so good at writing about fish that her boss encouraged her to write books. She wrote *Under the Sea Wind*, *The Sea Around Us*, and *The Edge of the Sea*.

In her books she wrote how everything in the oceans and on Earth is connected to everything else and to the environment. It was a new way to think about the world.

Now she was a famous author, so she had to give speeches and talk to newspaper reporters. She didn't like that. She was still shy.

At first when people read her books, many thought that a man must be the real author. They didn't think a woman could know so much about science. They were surprised to see the author was a small, slender, well-dressed woman with chestnut hair and blue-green eyes.

One day a woman wrote Rachel a letter saying that an airplane had sprayed the bug poison, DDT, over her yard to kill insects. Afterward, she found dead robins on her lawn, their claws drawn up to their breasts in agony. The DDT had killed them.

"Can't you do something to stop the spraying?" she wrote.

Rachel was already alarmed at the huge amounts of chemicals that were being sprayed onto the earth. New poisons had been invented for chemical warfare during the Second World War, and it turned out that some of the chemicals could kill weeds, bugs, and rodents. So now people sprayed them on lawns, gardens, farms, forests, school yards, parks, and golf courses. They didn't realize that the poisons were polluting the soil, seeping into drinking water, running off the land into oceans, and killing fish and wildlife.

As Rachel read the letter about the poisoned robins, she knew what she must do. She would write a book so full of facts that people would understand what was happening. They would demand changes.

Her best friend, Dorothy, warned her, "The companies that make insecticides will hate you if you write this book. They're rich and powerful. They'll do anything to turn people against you."

"I understand that, Dorothy," replied Rachel, "and I will be expecting it. But knowing what I do, there would be no peace for me if I kept silent. I could never again listen happily to a thrush song."

She named her book *Silent Spring*, because there would be no bird songs if all the birds are killed by insect poisons. There will be no people left to hear them either, because those chemicals could end all life on Earth.

As she worked on *Silent Spring*, she learned that she had cancer, and it could not be cured. She was in pain and sometimes could hardly walk. Now she raced against time to finish her book.

Some things that Rachel wrote about in *Silent Spring:*

❧ The bald eagle, the symbol of the United States, was becoming extinct because DDT prevented the eagle's eggs from hatching.

❧ A chemical that was sprayed over many acres in Illinois to kill Japanese beetles had also killed thousands of squirrels, rabbits, muskrats, birds, and cats.

❧ Poisons actually make insects even harder to kill, because the ones who survive then mate and breed "super bugs." This is called becoming resistant to the chemical. Then chemists have to make even deadlier poisons.

❧ A chemical such as DDT does not just disappear after it is sprayed. DDT sprayed on alfalfa shows up in cow's milk after the cow eats the alfalfa. Rain carries it into rivers and out into oceans, where it gets into fish, oysters, crabs, penguins, seals, and other creatures. DDT sprayed in the United States ends up in Iceland, Japan, the Arctic, the Antarctic— everywhere.

When Rachel finished *Silent Spring* in 1962, she cried with relief. All she wanted to do was rest.

Her book shocked the whole world. The companies who made the insecticides were enraged. They fumed, "Rachel Carson is just a nature nut!" They made up lies about her and spent thousands and thousands of dollars trashing her on the radio and on TV, and in newspapers and magazines.

So Rachel couldn't just rest after all. She had to go on television to debate men from the government and big chemical companies. This was a hard thing for a shy person to do, especially since she was sick.

She did it because she knew that TV would reach even more people than her book. Her voice was soft, but firm. She knew exactly what she needed to say and how to say it.

She warned, "People talk about conquering nature, but people are a part of nature. What we do to nature we do to ourselves. The war against nature is a war against our- selves."

President John F. Kennedy read *Silent Spring*. He called for a special committee of top scientists to study the facts and decide who was right —Rachel Carson or her enemies.

Rachel Carson

USA 17c

"What we do to nature we do to ourselves."

The committee announced that everything Rachel had written was true.

Congress passed new laws to protect the environment. One law banned DDT in the United States. That saved eagles from extinction. People began to think about taking care of the Earth.

Rachel was awarded many medals, but she was too sick to go to all the places that wanted to honor her.

One day she and Dorothy sat on a rocky cliff in Maine, watching monarch butterflies migrate to Mexico for the winter. They knew that those butterflies would not live to return to Maine, but their offspring would come. That was the natural life cycle of a butterfly. Rachel thought about that. Later she wrote, "Those fluttering bits of life taught me…that it is a natural and not unhappy thing that a life comes to an end. I have deep happiness in knowing that." Soon after that she died.

Rachel Carson will always be remembered for her courage in protecting the Earth, and for showing us how we are part of a wonderful web of life.

People did not weave the web of life,
We are merely a strand in it.
Whatever we do to the web,
We do to ourselves.

— attributed to Chief Seattle, 1854

Flee Flea! (safely)

Help Carry on the Work to Protect Earth!

Some flea collars, flea bombs and flea powders contain nerve poisons that can harm pets. Here's how to get rid of fleas without poisons:

Drown the fleas by giving your pet a long bath with just plain soap, not a flea shampoo.

Comb your pet with a fine-tooth flea comb (metal, not plastic). When you see fleas in the comb, dunk them a bowl of water with soap or alcohol in it.

Never crush fleas with your fingers because fleas might be carrying diseases.

Vacuum the house often to get rid of flea eggs, larvae and pupae. Seal the vacuum bag in plastic and put it out in the hot sun to kill everything you vacuumed up.

Use a cover on your pet's bedding, so you can wash it often.

Make a non-poisonous flea killer. Ask an adult to help.
1. Cut up 2 lemons, skin and all, into chunks.

2. Pour 2 cups of boiling water over this. Let stand overnight.

3. Sponge it on your pet.

WEB of LIFE

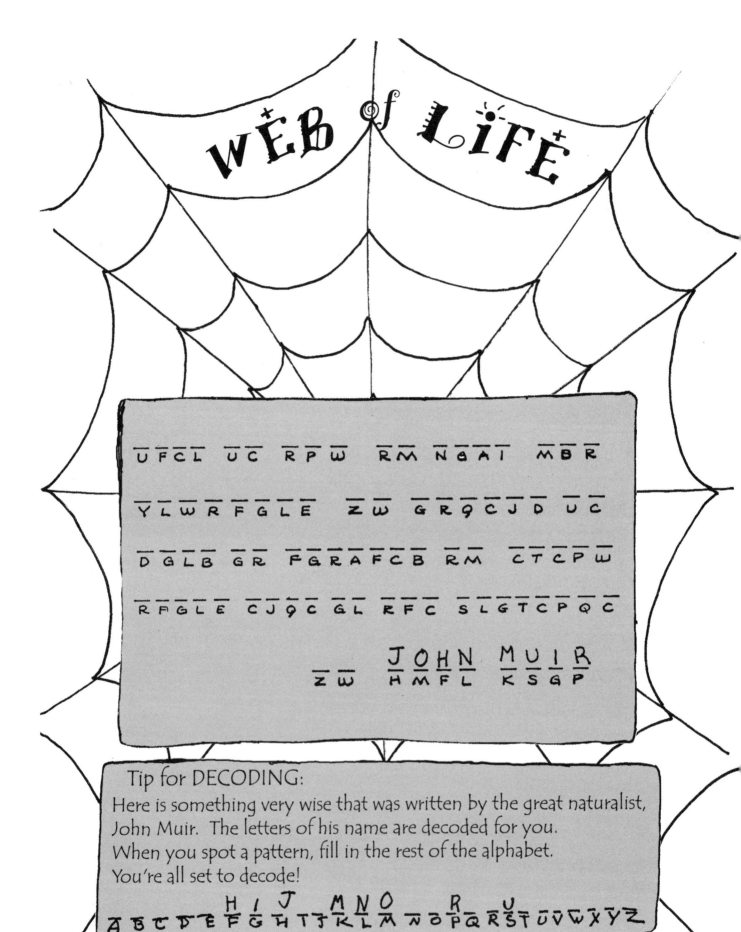

UFCL UC RPW RM NGAT MBR

YLWRFGLE ZW GRQCJD UC

DGLB GR FGRAFCB RM CTCPW

RFGLE CJQC GL RFC SLGTCPQC

ZW JOHN MUIR
(ZW) (HMFL) (KSGP)

Tip for DECODING:
Here is something very wise that was written by the great naturalist, John Muir. The letters of his name are decoded for you.
When you spot a pattern, fill in the rest of the alphabet.
You're all set to decode!

```
      H  I  J     M  N  O        R        U
A  B  C  D  E  F  G  H  I  J  K  L  M  N  O  P  Q  R  S  T  U  V  W  X  Y  Z
```

Awesome #5

The Ancestor of All Your Ancestors Was Invisible

Before you were born, you grew inside your mother's womb for nine months. After you had grown for 26 days, you looked like one of the embryos (EM-bree-O) below. These are the embryos of a bird, cow, tortoise, pig, human, and rabbit. But which is which?

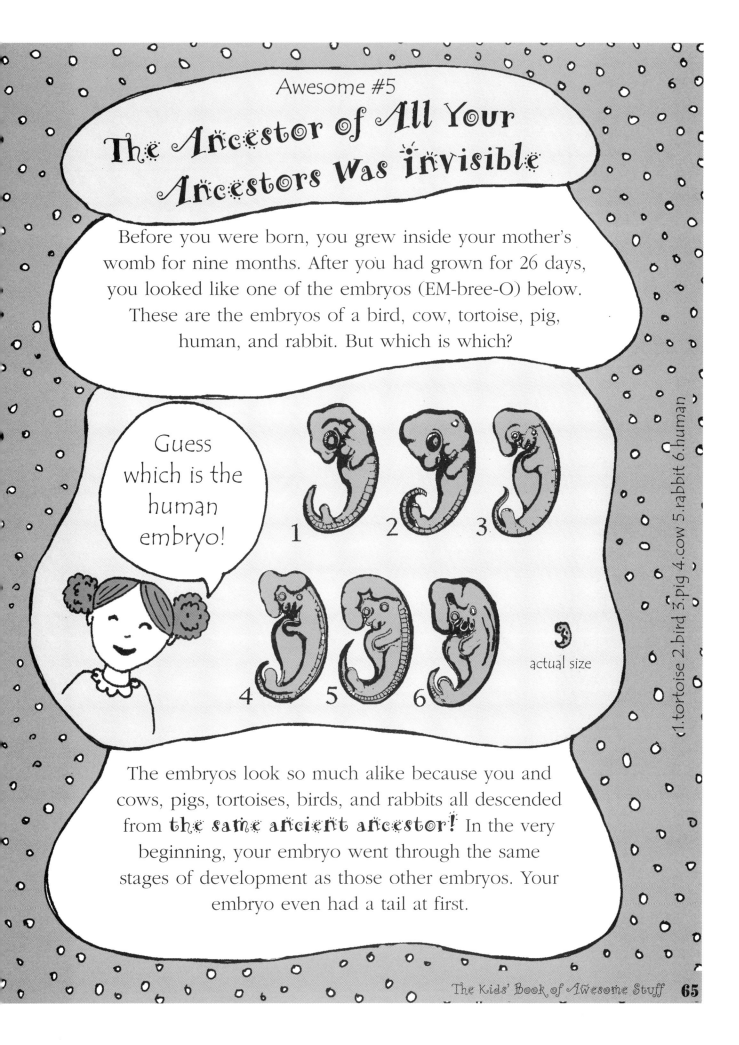

Guess which is the human embryo!

1   2   3

4   5   6

actual size

(1.tortoise 2.bird 3.pig 4.cow 5.rabbit 6.human

The embryos look so much alike because you and cows, pigs, tortoises, birds, and rabbits all descended from **the same ancient ancestor!** In the very beginning, your embryo went through the same stages of development as those other embryos. Your embryo even had a tail at first.

WHY Your Hand Has FIVE Fingers

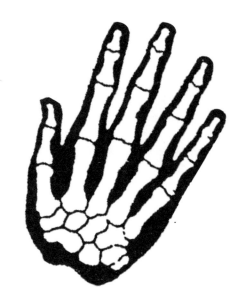

How many "fingers" are in:
—the wing of a bat?
—the forefoot of a mole?
—the flipper of a porpoise?
—the forefoot of a duckbilled platypus?

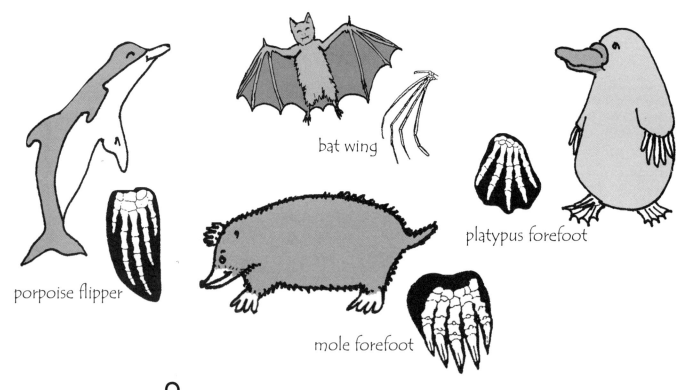

bat wing

platypus forefoot

porpoise flipper

mole forefoot

The five-finger bone design was around long before there were any humans on Earth. *You* and moles, bats, porpoises, and duckbilled platypuses all have five finger bones because you are *all* mammals. Mammals are animals that nurse their young, and all mammals are descended from…

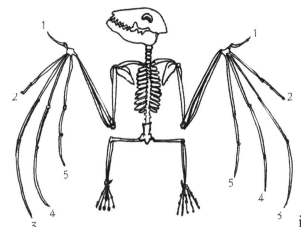

...the same ancient ancestor!

You can see the bat's enormously long fingers —five on each hand. All the fingers, except the thumb, act as supports for its wings. The skin over the wings stretches between the fingers and the legs. You can also see the five toes on each foot.

Your Ancient Genes

When you started your life as a little speck, you inherited **genes** from each of your parents. Genes are like beads strung on threads, so very tiny that they can only be seen under a microscope. They contain thousands of bits of information about you, such as whether you will have curly hair or straight, dark skin or light, be short or tall. Maybe you look like your mother in some ways, or like your father or an aunt or uncle or grandparent. That's because you received a mixture of genes passed on from your parents

I've got my granddad's eyes!

I've got my mother's spots!

and their parents and ancestors.

Every living thing, whether it is an oak tree or worm or jellyfish, has genes that contain information on what it will be.

You inherit your family's genes, but you also inherit genes from the far, far distant past. They are like many of the genes in other kinds of living things.

Mine, too!

Some of our genes are the same as YOUR genes!

Most of your genes—98%—are like the genes in a chimpanzee. In fact, your blood and chimp blood are so much alike that you and a chimpanzee could give each other blood transfusions.

You, yeast, mice, radishes, chimpanzees, and fruit flies have some genes alike because all living things are descended from **the same ancient ancestor!**

So who was that very first ancestor?

The Ancestor of us all was...

...a single bacterial cell floating in a warm, shallow sea, 3 1/2 billion years ago.

All other life developed from this first, simple cell. Each new kind of life was related to the kind that came before it in a long, long chain of life. This changing of one form of life into another over time is called *evolution*.

We know bacteria were the first living things on the planet because scientists have found their fossils in Earth's oldest rocks. Each bacterium was just one cell, so tiny that it was invisible. You need a microscope to see their fossils.

The ancient bacteria looked like the bacteria that are alive today.

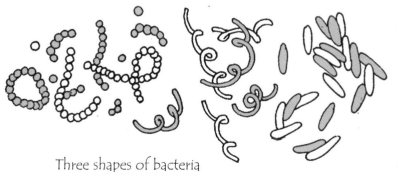

Three shapes of bacteria

The Only Life For HOW Long?

Bacteria were the *only* life on Earth for 2 billion years. That's 2,000,000,000 years.

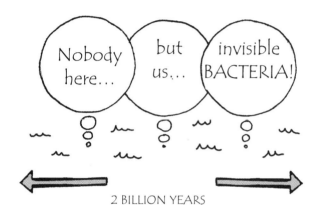

2 BILLION YEARS

Planet Earth began as a molten lava fireball. After it cooled down enough for rocks to harden and for rain to fall, the first life—bacteria—appeared. Meteorites were blasting the planet, volcanoes were erupting everywhere, and the air was thick with poisonous gases.

Yet the bacteria lived. There was no oxygen in the air for them to breathe, but those early bacteria didn't need it. They breathed sulfur and iron. Oxygen would have killed them.

The Mystery of all Mysteries

How did the very FIRST life begin?

?????

No one knows for sure. The warm seawater was like a soup of chemicals. Was life created when lightning zapped molecules of carbon, nitrogen, and hydrogen—the chemical building blocks of life? Did life start in sea spray? Or in superheated water spouting from undersea volcanoes? (Bacteria still live in such places, breathing iron and eating a diet of hot chemicals from the water.) Did a comet or meteorite carry chemical mixes for life to Earth?

comet

It's even possible that life began several times, but was killed off by meteorites. Some scientists think life could be continually springing up on planets throughout the Universe.

A Mutant's Invention

Bacteria reproduce by splitting in half. First, the cell grows double in size, makes a copy of its genes, and then divides to become two cells. Each new cell now has a set of identical genes, so they are twin cells—exactly alike. But sometimes the cell makes a mistake when it copies its genes. Then the new cell is different. It's a mutant.

A mutant bacterium invented photosynthesis. Now it didn't have to find food to eat, like the other bacteria did. It could make its own food by using energy from the sun. It captured sun energy with a green chemical called chlorophyll.

A blue-green bacteria, called cyanobacteria (sy-AN-o-bacteria), evolved from the mutant bacterium. When cyanobacteria made their food, they breathed out leftover oxygen. This oxygen brought instant death to most of the other bacteria. Many kinds became extinct. Some survived by staying in places that oxygen couldn't reach, such as deep mud and scalding geysers. Cyanobacteria gradually spread across the Earth's surface, wherever there was water and sunlight. As they grew, they made more and more oxygen. New species of bacteria evolved that could stand the oxygen, and use it. Slowly, slowly, cyanobacteria made so much oxygen that the air all over Earth changed. Now, new kinds of life that needed to breathe oxygen could evolve. Animals, plants, fungi, birds, fish, insects, and people could exist. And YOU.

geyser

The oxygen also formed a shield, called the ozone layer, in the atmosphere that protected living things from the sun's dangerous ultraviolet light. That made it safe

Just think... those invisible green specks of life changed the whole world!

THANKS cyano!

for creatures to move out of water and onto the land.

None of us would be here today without cyanobacteria! And that's not all. We can thank cyano-bacteria for green plants because:

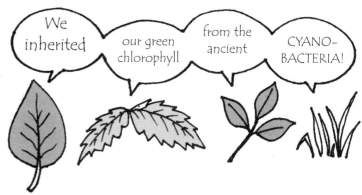

We inherited our green chlorophyll from the ancient CYANO-BACTERIA!

Cyanobacteria are still around. They're among the organisms that form green slime, the kind on the sides of a fish tank. Who would ever guess that slimy stuff has ancestors that made it possible for you to live in this world?

You Had Sea Ancestors Before Land Ancestors

At first every living thing in the world was in the sea. Nothing flew in the air. Nothing roamed on the land.

Millions and millions of years passed before new kinds of life evolved that were bigger than just one cell. The first life with many cells was a seaweed, and then animals such as jellyfish, sponges, sea worms, and corals evolved.

Now certain cells could do special jobs, instead of one cell doing everything. Jellyfish evolved with nerve cells and muscle cells.

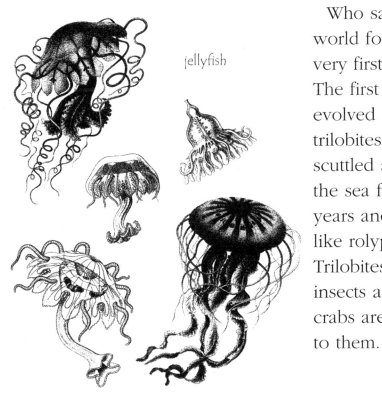

jellyfish

Worms Had Your Body Design First!

Sea worms were the first creatures to evolve with a body design that has a head and a tube where food comes in one end and out the other.

That's the same basic body design that you have! This design was quite different from jellyfish, which are more like a floating stomach.

a fancy sea worm

Who Had the First Eyes in the World?

Who saw the world for the very first time? The first eyes evolved in trilobites (TRY-low-bites). Trilobites scuttled along the bottom of the sea for 300 million years and could roll up like rolypoly bugs. Trilobites are extinct, but insects and horseshoe crabs are related to them.

trilobites

horseshoe crab
a relative of trilobites

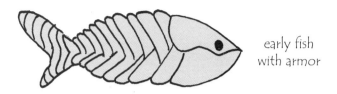
early fish
with armor

Who had The First Backbone?

Fish had the first backbones. A backbone had to evolve before there could be any *you*.

Early fish were covered with heavy, bony armor. In time, the armor evolved into lightweight scales.

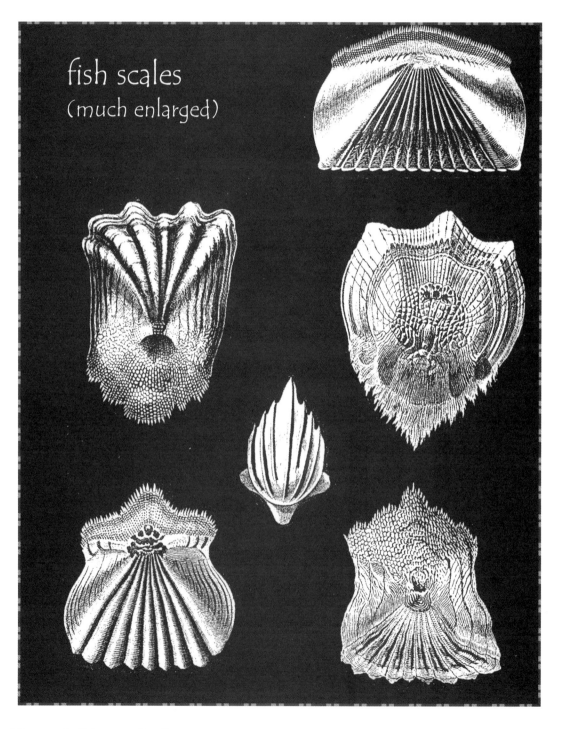

fish scales
(much enlarged)

The Land Was Empty Until...

Can you guess what kind of life was the very first to move from sea to land? It was a flat moss that clung to the water's edge, over 400 million years ago.

The first animals appeared on land a few million years after the first plant. These animal pioneers were scorpions, spiders, centipedes, millipedes, and an insect like a silverfish.

The greatest danger for plants and animals moving onto land from the sea was the risk of drying out in the glaring sun.

Drying meant dying.

Plants that left water invented ways to keep themselves wet on the inside. They evolved thick stems containing tubes to carry water up to all their cells.

The first animals that moved to land evolved a waterproof covering, and carried seawater inside themselves. You inherited a waterproof bag—your skin—and you carry water inside you.

Scorpion –an ancient pioneer on land

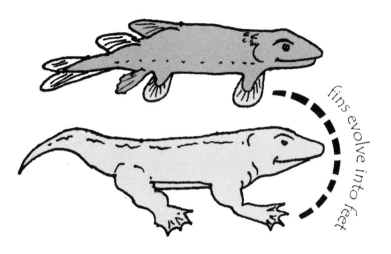

fins evolve into feet

Yea for the Fish with Four Feet!

At the time when life moved onto land, the only animals in the world with backbones were fish. Animals with backbones might just have stayed in water forever, if lobe-fin fish had not run into trouble.

The water in the ponds and streams where they lived was slowly drying because Earth's climate was warming up. Luckily, lobe-fin fish had strong bones in each fin, and lungs for breathing in air as well as gills for breathing in water. As ponds dried to puddles, the lobe-fins dragged themselves on their stubby fins across the mud to larger puddles. When the water was too muddy for them to take in oxygen through their gills, they could prop themselves up on their fins to gulp in air.

The ones with the strongest bones in their fins could go farther between ponds, reach the most food, and live to have the most young. They fit in best with the drying climate. They passed on their genes for strong fin bones to their young. Sometimes mutations of genes made the fin bones longer and more spread out. The fish with those mutations survived best. Over many, many generations, their fins evolved into feet.

1

2

3

4

When one kind of living thing survives because it fits in best with its environment, this process is called "natural selection". Evolution works through natural selection.

A fish with four feet evolved into the first **amphibian**. Amphibians grow up in water, but live on land as adults. They return to water to lay eggs. Frogs are amphibians. So are salamanders.

The Big iF...

IF lobe-fin fish had not evolved into amphibians, there would be no *reptiles*, like turtles and alligators. Reptiles evolved from amphibians.

IF there had been no reptiles, there would be no mammals, like cats, cows and people. Mammals evolved from reptiles. There would have been NO YOU!

And no ME! I'm a mammal too!

Dinosaurs evolved from a tiny 4-inch reptile.

You And The Chain Of Life...

Birds evolved from dinosaurs. *Mammals* and dinosaurs evolved at about the same time.

The first mammals were rat-sized. They scurried about, hunting for seeds and insects, hiding away under bushes from dinosaurs who would make a meal of them. Those mammals stayed small for almost 200 million years, until the dinosaurs became extinct. Once the dinosaurs died out, mammals had a chance to grow larger and evolve into many different species —over 5,000 species.

Mammal mothers evolved a way to make milk in their own bodies to feed their babies.

Bad luck for dinosaurs, but... Good luck for us mammals

Mammals also evolved a way to stay warm and active in cold places. Reptiles become sluggish when it's cold because their temperature matches the temperature of the air or water around them. They're cold-blooded. You're a warm-blooded mammal, and so your temperature always stays the same—about 98.6 degrees fahrenheit (unless you're sick) —whether it's hot or cold outside.

Four-winged dinosaur

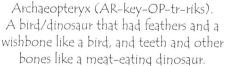

Archaeopteryx (AR-key-OP-tr-riks). A bird/dinosaur that had feathers and a wishbone like a bird, and teeth and other bones like a meat-eating dinosaur.

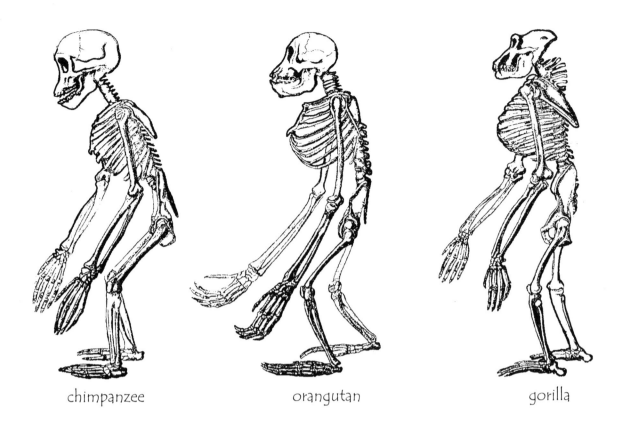

chimpanzee

orangutan

gorilla

Apes are close mammal relatives. You're not descended from an ape. You just had the same ancestor way, way back in time.

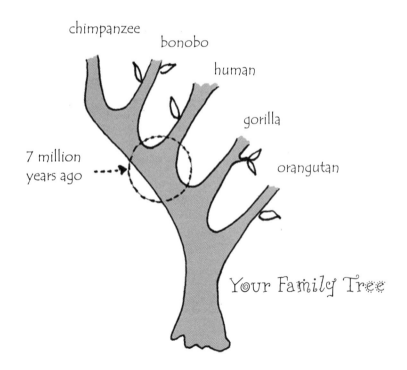

chimpanzee

bonobo

human

gorilla

orangutan

7 million years ago

Your Family Tree

The Same Ancestor

Humans, chimpanzees and bonobos all had the same ancestor around 7 million years ago, but then each group branched off and evolved separately. Humans and dinosaurs had the same reptile ancestor around 300 million years ago. So dinosaurs are more distant relatives than chimps and bonobos.

Gorillas, chimpanzees, and orangutans are not really all the same size, as they are shown here. Their skeletons are pictured the same size to make it easier for you to see how they are alike and different.

Humans Came Late to the Planet

Yardstick Timeline for Earth

Suppose a yardstick was a timeline for the whole time that Earth has existed. One end of the yardstick would represent the time when Earth formed in the solar system. The other end of the yardstick would be right now, the present time.

Your First Human Ancestors Had Dark Skin

Whether your skin is dark or light, everybody's earliest human ancestors were dark-skinned. That's because the very first humans in the world evolved in Africa, where it's hot and sunny. Their dark skin protected them against the sun's dangerous ultraviolet rays. Early humans that moved to cooler, northern climates evolved lighter skin over time. Light skin can take in extra sunlight, which we need to make vitamin D.

Africa

Dozens of Cousins!

And all from the same ancient ancestor! You are related to every plant and every animal and every bacterium that ever lived on Earth. Some of your relatives are distant, like ferns and jellyfish. Others are closer, like chimpanzees, but they are *all* your relatives.

Can you spot 27 rainforest cousins?

Color them if you wish.

No form of life is better than another, just different. Each has a part to play in the web of life.

Every kind of life evolved over billions
of years from a simple beginning.
And now...there is YOU.
YOU...who once started as a tiny speck.
YOU...who are here because of
all the life that came before you.
And in all this time there has
never been anyone else like YOU.
And there never will be again.
YOU are a once-in-a-universe event.

YOU are AWESOME!

The Stream of Life

The same stream of life that runs

through my veins night and day

runs through the world.

It is the same life that shoots in joy

through the dust of the earth

in the many blades of grass

and leaves and flowers.

It is the same life that is rocked

in the ocean-cradle of birth and of death,

in the coming and going of the tides.

I feel the life-throb of all the ages

dancing in my blood this moment.

—Rabindranath Tagore (adapted)
Hindu poet

You Live on a Speck in a Spinning Spiral

The spiral you live in whirls around and around like a gigantic pinwheel in outer space—and you're whirling along with it!

The spiral is the Milky Way galaxy. We can't take its picture, because we're all on a speck INSIDE it! But if we *could* take a picture, it would look very much like this photo of the Whirlpool Galaxy.

Side view of the Sombrero spiral galaxy.

The Milky Way Galaxy

is thin and flat, like a frisbee, only with a bulge in the middle

FRISBEE

Side view of a frisbee

What's Inside Your Spinning Spiral?
...Besides You & the Speck?...

Answer: 100 billion stars plus great clouds of hydrogen, helium, dust, and *lots of empty space.*

The Sun is a medium-sized, ordinary star among all those 100 billion stars. At the core of the Milky Way galaxy is a black hole. Anything that funnels down into the black hole disappears.

Even though you live on a speck inside the galaxy, you can sometimes see a rim of it—a border—in the night sky. It looks like a fuzzy path of light stretching across the heavens. You can see it best in July or August, away from city lights.

Lucky for us, gravity holds it all together!

What would you have named the Milky Way?

When you look at the Milky Way through a telescope you can see that it is made of stars. What looks like a cloud, like spilled milk, is really millions of distant stars.

But if you had lived long ago, before telescopes were invented, what might you have imagined this mysterious path of light to be? What would you have called it?

Ancient Names
for the Milky Way from
Far Corners of the World

Long, Blue Cloud-Eating Shark
Road Made of Milk
Great Serpent
River of Light
Silver Street
Backbone of Night

I would have named it

Salt stars

The Milky Way Galaxy in a Box of Salt

100 billion stars is such a HUGE number that it's is hard for us to imagine. Here's something you can do to help you understand the almost unbelievable number of stars in our Milky Way galaxy.

Materials:

* a regular box of SALT. (l lb., 10 oz. box)
* a plain dark cloth to spread on the floor or on a table top. You need to cover a space of about three feet by three feet.

Directions:

1. Pour the salt on top of the cloth in a big SPIRAL. Use up the whole box. Make the salt thickest at the center of the spiral.

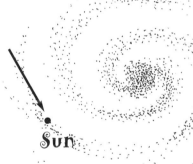

Sun

2. **Imagine that each single grain of salt is a STAR.**

3. Now choose one of the salt grains about 2/3 of the way out from the center on a rim of the spiral. Call that salt grain the SUN. Mark it in some way if you wish.

4. And now imagine that this whole spiral is turning counter-clockwise. The star that is the Sun is turning with it. (So are you and the Earth.)

Picture the Sun making one complete circle around the center of the Milky Way galaxy, back to its starting place. That trip took 226 million years. Dinosaurs would have been roaming the Earth the last time the Sun was where it is right now.

5. And finally, try to imagine 100 billion galaxies out there in space. If the whole Universe were a snowstorm, each galaxy would be like a single, swirling snowflake in the storm.

You can clean up the salt by shaking the cloth into a wastebasket.

Galaxies in Outer Space

You are looking deep, deep

into space in this photo, named *Hubble Deep Field*.

Every dot and smudge you see is an entire galaxy,

except for two stars from our own Milky Way

galaxy. A star looks like a spot

with a cross of light on it.

A "Ghost" Universe

Did you know…light from the very farthest galaxies in the Hubble Deep Field photo took 10 billion years to reach Earth?

Light travels fast—186,000 miles per second—but those galaxies are so far away that it still takes billions of years for their light to get here. Their light started out long before there even *was* a Planet Earth. Earth has only been around for four and a half billion years.

Sort of like looking at a GHOST universe?

The light from this star (WR124) reaches Earth in 15,000 years. The star is the white center and is ejecting hot clumps of gas.

Jupiter's light reaches Earth in an hour.

Mars's light gets here in a few minutes.

We see galaxies as they looked when their light first started speeding through space—not how they look today. But when you see the Sun, you see it as it looked only eight minutes ago. That's how long it takes for the Sun's light to travel to Earth.

Light from stars takes from one to 100,000 years to arrive at Earth, depending on how far away the star is. You might even see starlight from a star that no longer exists!

When you view the heavens, you are looking back in time. Telescopes are like time machines. They let you look at galaxies, stars and planets as they looked in the past.

A Speck inside the Milky Way Galaxy

PLANET EARTH

YOU and Planet Earth are spinning about 1,000 miles an hour as you hurtle around a star—the Sun.

The Dizzy Rounds

Guaranteed to Make You Dizzy!

Make your body spin around and circle at the same time, as if you were the Earth circling the sun.

All you need is some space and a friend.

1. Your friend, the Sun, stands in the center of the space.
2. Tilt your head, tipping it to the side, because the Earth is tilted.
3. Turn like a top—but not too fast! That's the Earth rotating. When you face your friend, it's day. When your back is to your friend, it's night.
4. Now, while you are rotating, move in a circle around your friend, the Sun, at the same time. That's the Earth revolving. Each time you revolve completely around your friend, a year has passed. Did you manage to tilt, rotate and revolve all the way around the Sun?
5. Now trade places with your friend. You be the Sun, your friend can be the Earth.

It's Always Sunrise Somewhere

When you see the Sun rise in the east and set in the west, it seems as if the Sun is moving across the sky from east to west. But that's not what is really happening. It's the Earth that's moving, not the Sun. The Earth spins round and round from west to east. As it rotates, it carries you forward, toward the Sun.

It is always sunrise somewhere...
On seas and continents and islands,
Each in it's turn as the round Earth rolls.

John Muir

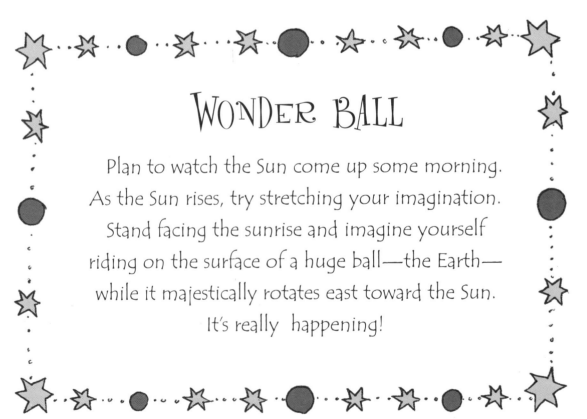

WONDER BALL

Plan to watch the Sun come up some morning. As the Sun rises, try stretching your imagination. Stand facing the sunrise and imagine yourself riding on the surface of a huge ball—the Earth—while it majestically rotates east toward the Sun. It's really happening!

SHADOW GUIDE

Here's How It Works:

1. Push a straight stick upright into the ground in a sunny place where it can throw a shadow. (Pick a spot where the stick will remain in sunlight for several hours.)

2. Put a small stone on the ground to mark the spot where the stick's shadow ends.

3. Wait about an hour. By that time, the shadow will have moved a little to the east. Put another small stone on the ground where the stick's shadow now ends. Your first stone is WEST. Your second stone is EAST.

4. Now stand in front of the stick, facing the stones. Place your left foot so that the tip of your shoe touches the first stone. Place your right foot so that the tip of your shoe touches the second stone.

5. You will be facing exactly NORTH. Behind you will be SOUTH.

6. Try this out first at home, so you'll remember what to do if you're ever lost.

1.

2.

3.

Star Traveler

Invite your family and friends to join you for some star travel on a clear, starry night. It's easy! Bring blankets or sleeping bags, so that all of you can lie on your backs and look up at the splendor above.

Surprise your star-gazing companions with these starry facts:

★ By the time 5 minutes have passed, the spinning Earth has taken you 87 miles to the east.

★ In those 5 minutes, you have whirled with the Earth around the Sun for 5,500 miles.

★ And in that same time, you, the Earth, and the Sun, have journeyed 50,000 miles around the Milky Way galaxy! That's 166 miles per second, or 600,000 miles per hour!

You are a star-traveler, spinning, circling within circles in the cosmos

A Time When People Didn't Know

There was once a time when you could be put in a dungeon or killed, if you dared to think the Earth circled the Sun.

For centuries people believed that the Earth stood still, and the Sun revolved around it. After all, when you see the Sun come up, travel across the sky and go down, it looks as though the Sun is going around the Earth. And Earth doesn't *feel* like it's moving.

Many people believed that certain Bible verses were proof that the Sun circled the Earth, and that God created the Earth as the center of the Universe.

Everyone thought the planets also circled Earth, but no one could figure out why the planets followed such peculiar paths. Especially Mars. It doubled back on itself like a pretzel. The path of Mars was a riddle in the sky.

Then around the time of Christopher Columbus, a Polish astronomer named Nicolaus Copernicus (Kuh-PER-nuh-kus) asked himself: "What if I could view the paths of the planets from some other place in space, instead of looking at them from Earth?"

So he imagined he was standing on the Sun. Then he realized that if the planets were actually circling the Sun, instead of the Earth, their paths made perfect sense.

Using mathematics, he worked out an idea that seemed utterly unbelievable: the Earth is just another planet! It goes around the Sun, spinning the whole time. That's what makes it seem as if the Sun moves across the sky. It's really the Earth that is moving!

Mars didn't really travel a pretzel

path after all. It just looked that way from Earth, because Mars and Earth were both moving at the same time, each in a different path of its own.

Copernicus told his friends about his ideas, and wrote them down, but he refused to publish them in a book. He was afraid that people would laugh at him.

His ideas sounded crazy. They were new, hard to understand, and he had no way to prove them. People would be shocked to think of Earth as just another planet.

He also knew that he might be accused of going against the Bible.

But his friends were so excited about his ideas that they spread the news all over Europe.

Actors put on a play about Copernicus that made him look just as ridiculous as he had feared. Leaders of the Protestant religions said, "Copernicus is a fool!

He's turning astronomy upside down! No one should dare believe Copernicus over the Bible." However, some important leaders of the Roman Catholic Church took Copernicus's side.

When Copernicus grew old and knew he was dying, he finally agreed to let his friends publish his book. He clutched the book in his hands for the first time, just as he died. The year was 1543.

Fifty years passed. An Italian scientist, named Galileo, read Copernicus's book. He thought Copernicus might be right, but there was no way to prove it. Galileo didn't know, then, that he would be the one to discover the proof.

Around the same time, a Dutchman had invented a spyglass that showed things closer, but upside down and fuzzy. Galileo used his design to create the world's first telescope.

Everyone will laugh at me!

COPERNICUS

He pointed his telescope at the night sky. It was 1609. He was stunned at what he saw. The moon had mountains, craters, and deep valleys. It was not a smooth crystal ball as everyone had always believed.

He peered at the Milky Way and saw that it was made of many stars. Most astonishing of all, the planet Jupiter had four moons circling it. That meant that everything in the heavens did not move around Earth. And if moons could move around a planet, then planets could move around the Sun.

Galileo quickly wrote a book about his discoveries. He sent a copy of it and a telescope to all the kings and princes of Europe, and to leaders of the Catholic Church. Soon he was famous.

But times were changing. New ideas now seemed dangerous to the Catholic Church. It was becoming more and more strict. In those days,

Copernicus was right!

it had the power to condemn anyone to prison or death for not believing its teachings. The Church taught that the Earth was not a planet, and the Earth did not move. The Church banned the writings of Copernicus in 1616. No one was allowed to read his book anymore, or say that his ideas were true. It became a serious crime to say the Earth moved around the Sun.

So Galileo kept silent about Copernicus for years. But when he was an old man, he decided to write a book about a group of friends arguing together for and against Copernicus's ideas. That way he would not be giving his own opinion, and Copernicus's ideas would not be forgotten. The trouble was that the arguments on Copernicus's side were so good, that the Church leaders grew furious.

A good friend of Galileo had become the new Pope. The Pope was the head of the Church, and also the highest ruler of the land. Galileo hoped his friend would keep him safe.

But Galileo had many enemies who were jealous of him, and they turned the Pope against him. Galileo was ordered to go to Rome to stand trial before ten judges in the Pope's court. He collapsed in fear, but he had to go.

The judges ruled: "GUILTY! You are guilty for holding a belief that is false to Holy Scripture. You are guilty for believing that the Earth is not the center of the Universe." To save himself from death, Galileo knelt and confessed to being wrong. In his heart he knew he was right.

The judges sentenced Galileo to a dungeon for the rest of his life.

But the Pope changed the sentence to house arrest. Galileo's home was guarded night and day, and he could never leave it. He became blind, but with the help of his son and friends, he spent his last years writing an important book on a new science we now call physics.

Many years passed. Scientists built bigger and better telescopes. They discovered that the solar system was just a tiny part of an enormous spiral galaxy.

At first they thought this galaxy was the only galaxy in the Universe, with nothing but blackness beyond it.

Then an astronomer discovered other galaxies. So the Milky Way was not alone in the Universe, after all.

Over the centuries, people learned:

COSMIC CROSSWORD

The Earth is *not* the center of the solar system.

The solar system is *not* the center of the Milky Way galaxy.

The Milky Way galaxy is *not* the center of the Universe.

You're lucky enough to live in a time when you can know what people never used to know. And guess what, every answer to the Universe opens up new questions!

Across

1. The shape of the Milky Way galaxy is a _____

3. He was afraid people would laugh at him for believing that the Earth moved around the sun.

5. It takes the sun 226 million years to travel one complete circle around the center of the _____.

7. Great clouds of _____, helium and dust are in the Milky Way galaxy.

9. _____holds everything together in the galaxy.

11. The sun is an ordinary star among 100 _____ stars in the Milky Way galaxy.

12. Light from the Sun takes _____minutes to reach the Earth.

13. _____are like time machines, letting us look back in time.

Down

2. The first person in the world to see planets and the moon as they really were.

4. When the earth spins like a top, it is _____.

6. The Milky Way galaxy is thin and _____, with a bulge in the middle.

8. A year passes each time the Earth _____ completely around the Sun.

10. _____ travels at a speed of 186,000 miles per second.

12. Shadows made by the Sun's light move slowly _____ as the Earth rotates.

You are a child of the Universe, no less than the trees and stars; you have a right to be here.

From "Desiderata" by Max Ehrmann 1927

Draw yourself in the place that says "You" and write what you think about the universe in the word balloon.

You ⬆

The Kids' Book of Awesome Stuff

Hey kids, this is a short way of saying all the stuff in this book.

A Short But True Story of YOU

YOU are made of star-stuff.

YOU are related to every other living thing on Earth.

YOU breathe out a gas that gives life to plants, and plants breathe out a gas that gives life to YOU.

YOU are part of a wonderful web of life on a planet spinning in space.

When you die, someday, the elements of your body will become a part of clouds and crystals, seas and new living things.

YOU can think and wonder, love and learn.

YOU have the gift of life.

Bye, now.

i pledge
to take care of
Planet Earth

Signed ————————————

The Kids' Book of Awesome Stuff

Answers to all the puzzles:

page 17, Star-Stuff word search

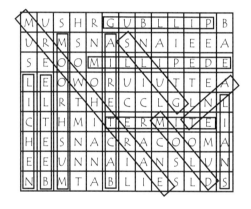

page 27, Super-Leaf Scramble:
1. *gas, smother*
2. *split, hydrogen*
3. *oxygen*
4. *carbon dioxide*
5. *sunlight*

p 34, We Recycle Dead Stuff
   word search

page 41, Recycling Elements
   If humans suddenly vanished from Earth, life on the planet would go on. But
   life on Earth would end without the: *bacteria* and *fungi*, and *worms*, and
   molds, and other recyclers that help make dead things *decay*.

page 45, Wanted
   "recycle"

page 64, Web of Life
   *"When we try to pick out anything by itself we find it hitched to everything
   else in the Universe."* by John Muir

page 99, Cosmic Crossword
   ACROSS: 1. spiral 3. Copernicus 5. galaxy 7. hydrogen 9. gravity 11. billion
         12. eight 13. telescopes
   DOWN: 2. Galileo 4. rotating 6. flat 8. revolves 10. light 12. east

Use this space for your own drawings, poems, thoughts and wonderings.

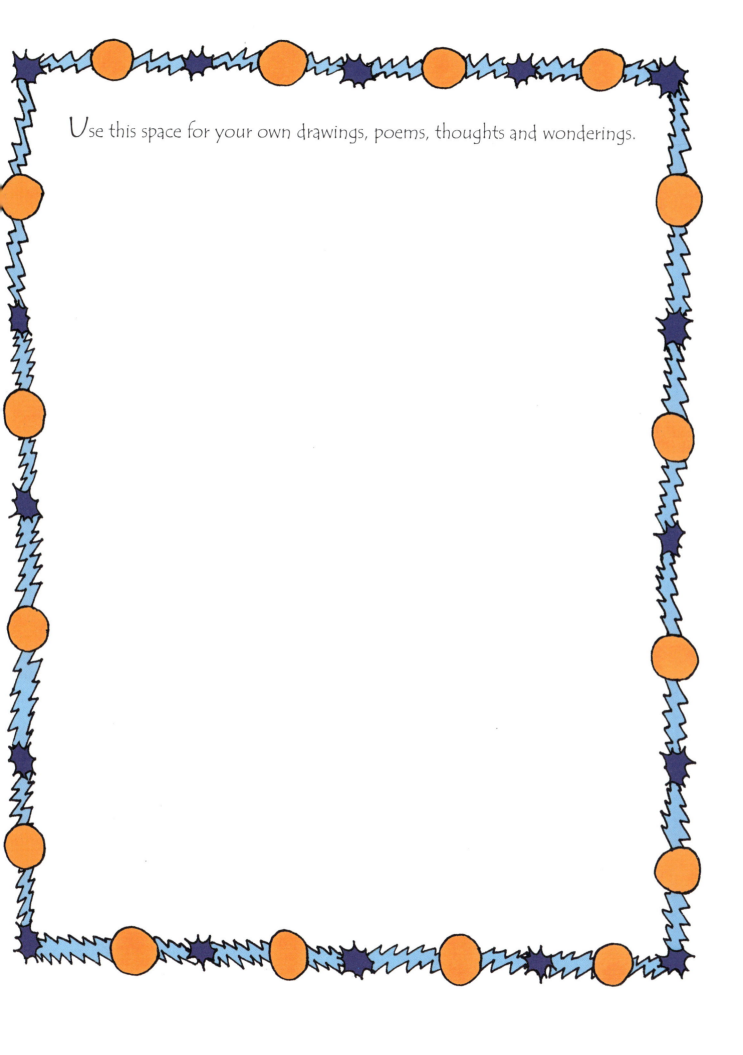

Use this space for your own drawings, poems, thoughts and wonderings.

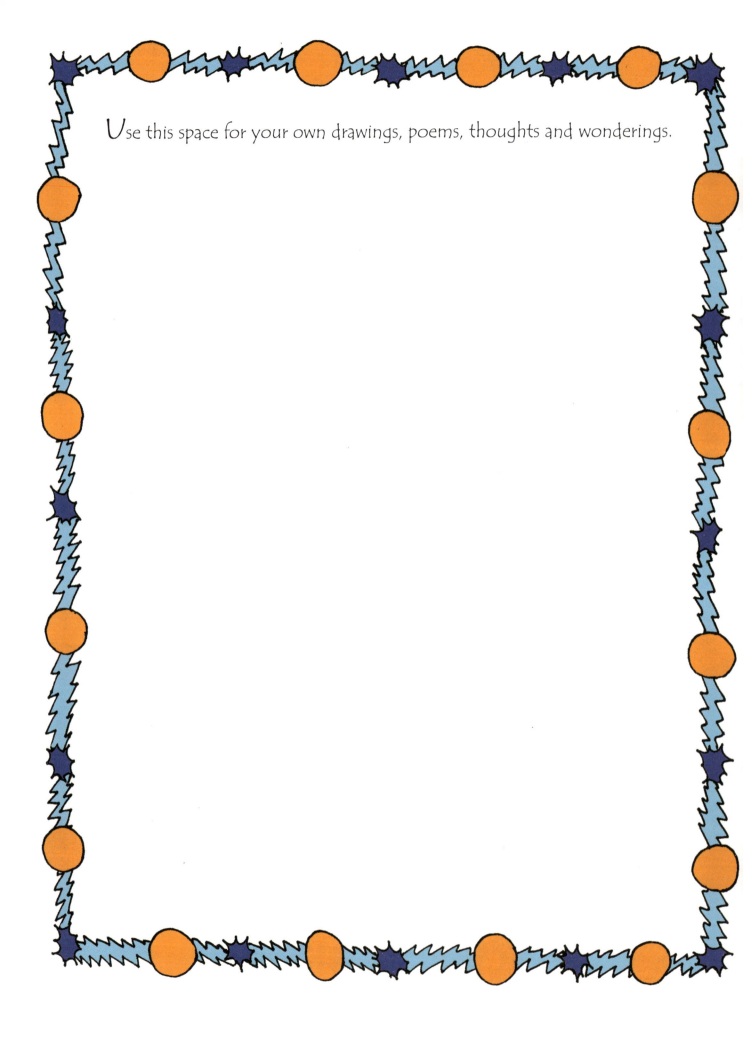

Use this space for your own drawings, poems, thoughts and wonderings.

Use this space for your own drawings, poems, thoughts and wonderings.

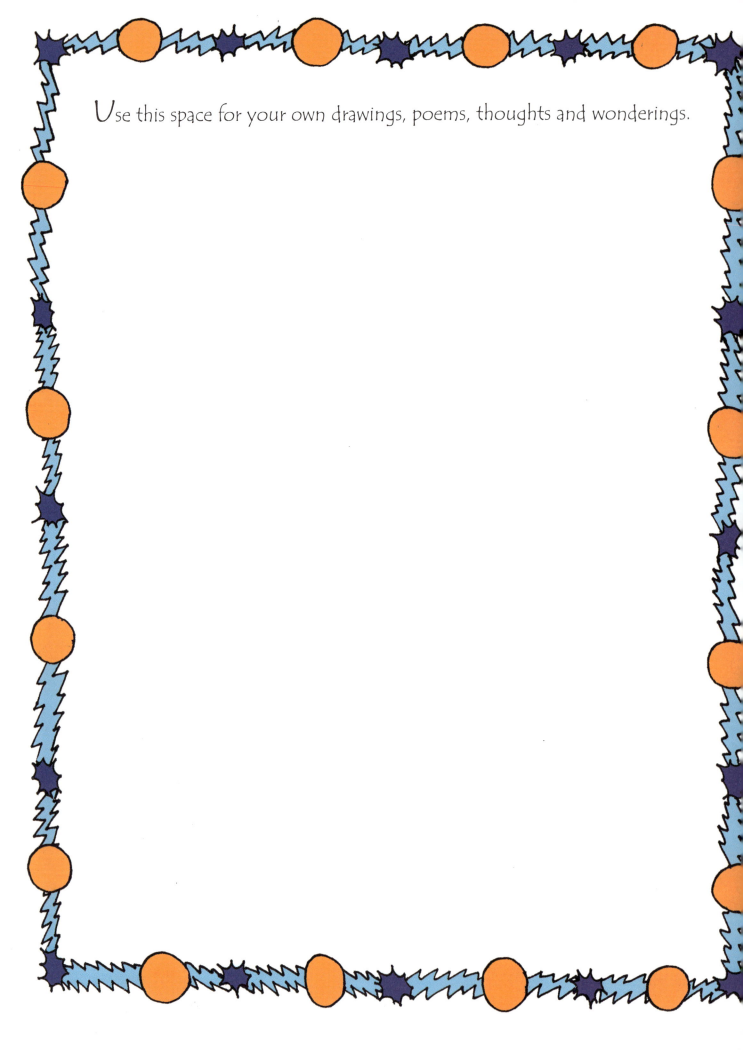

Use this space for your own drawings, poems, thoughts and wonderings.

Use this space for your own drawings, poems, thoughts and wonderings.

PHOTO CREDITS

Page 58
Rachel Carson as a Child, Reading to Her Dog: family photo, used by permission of Rachel Carson Council, Inc.

Page 59
Rachel Carson at Microscope, 1951: Brooks Studio, used by permission of Rachel Carson Council, Inc.

Page 54
Butterfly Scales, magnified
Used by permission of Dee Breger, Lamont-Doherty Earth Observatory

Page 85
Northern Milky Way
Used by permission of Jerry Lodriguess/Photo Researchers, Inc.

Page 90
Earth from space: Blue Marble West
Used by permission of NASA Goddard Space Flight Center, courtesy of SpaceImages.com

Hubble Space Telescope Photos
The following photos were taken by the Hubble Space Telescope, and appear courtesy of the National Aeronautics and Space Administration (NASA), the Space Telescope Science Institute (STScl), Association of Universities for Research in Astronomy (AURA) and the investigators listed below.

You can view the Hubble Space Telescope photos in this book and others at:
http://hubblesite.org/newscenter/newsdesk/archive

Page 3
Star N81: Mohammed Heydari-malayeri (Paris Observatory); NASA/ESA, 1998. Courtesy of SpaceImages.com.

Page 5
Ring Nebula (M57): H. Bond, K. Noll (STScl), 1999. Courtesy of SpaceImages.com.

Page 6
Cat's Eye Nebula (NGC 6543): J.P. Harrington (University of Maryland), K. Borkowski (North Carolina State University), 1995

Ant Nebula (MZ3): Hubble Heritage Team, ESA, 2001

Hourglass Nebula: R. Sahai, J. Trauger (Jet Propulsion Laboratory, 1996. Courtesy of SpaceImages.com.

Page 7
Cynus Loop supernova remnant: J.J. Hester (Arizona State University), 1993

Page 83
Whirlpool Galaxy: Hubble Heritage Team, 2001. Courtesy of SpaceImages.com.

Page 84
Sombrero galaxy: Hubble Heritage Team, 2003

Page 88
Hubble Deep Field: R. Williams (STScl), the Hubble Deep Field Team, 1996. Courtesy of SpaceImages.com.

Page 89
Star WR124: Yves Grosdidier and Anthony Moffat (University of Montreal), Gilles Joncas (University Laval), Agnew Acker (Observatoire de Strasbourg), 1998.

Jupiter: NASA, 1991

Mars: Hubble Heritage Team, 2001

PUZZLE CREDITS
Page 78, 79
Rainforest puzzle
Used by permission of My Earth 1991, Earthbooks, Incorporated

ACTIVITY CREDITS
Page 87
Salt Stars
Used by permission of Chet Raymo

Page 91
Dizzy Rounds
Used by permission of Cape Cod Museum of Natural History

ILLUSTRATION CREDITS

Pages 12, 13
Snowflakes, Frost
Derived from "Snow Crystals," W.A. Bentley and W.J. Humphreys, 1962, Dover
Publications

Page *71*
Jellyfish
Derived from "Art Forms in Nature," Ernst Haeckel, 1974, Dover Publications

ACKNOWLEDGEMENTS

My heartfelt gratitude to the following scientists who reviewed individual chapters for
scientific accuracy:

Dr. Michael Dolan, Department of Geosciences, University of Massachusetts

Dr. Russell Graham, Chief Curator, Denver Museum of Nature and Science

Dr. Stephen Ressel, Museum Director and Professor of Biology, College of the
Atlantic

Dr. Daniel Schnell, Director, Plant Biology Graduate Program, Department of
Biochemistry and Molecular Biology, University of Massachusetts

Roger Wrubel, Sanctuary Director, Habitat Education Center and Wildlife
Sanctuary, Massachusetts Audubon Society

Kimberly Smart, Teacher Education Specialist, North Carolina Museum of Natural
Sciences, Raleigh, NC